CW01021414

By the Naked Pear Tree

By The Naked Pear Tree

the trial of Lizzie Borden, a play in verse

michael thomas brimbau

PEARTREE PRESS: FALL RIVER, MASSACHUSETTS
2015

PearTree Press
P.O. Box 9585
Fall River, MA 02720
peartree-press.com

LIBRARY OF CONGRESS CONTROL NUMBER: **2015942845**

ISBN-13: 978-0-9908161-2-6

Printed in the United States of America on acid-free paper.

Book design by Stefani Koorey

Special thanks to Eugene Hosey and Pat Stafford

Cover Photograph: Stock illustration © bphillips
Frontis illustration: "Lizzie Faints Away," Police Gazette, 1893
Some of the poems included in By The Naked Pear Tree first appeared in The Hatchet: A Journal of Lizzie Borden & Victorian Studies

For Ada Jill Schneider,
lyricist and good friend.

Poetry Table of Contents

Poetry Table of Contents Continued

Introduction

TRIAL OF THE MIND AND HEART

In New Bedford, Massachusetts, an austere, noble coastal town of weathered sea captain homes and timeworn whaling ships, unfolds a case unlike any ever seen anywhere, let alone by a discreet, New England Yankee community.

Here a woman in her early thirties, named Lizzie Andrew Borden, is being accused of killing her elderly father and aging stepmother with a hatchet. The crime was committed a few miles away in the not-so-sleepy town of Fall River, Massachusetts. As decades unfold, it would become the case that never ends. After all, Victorian ladies just don't go around angrily mincing their parents with a hatchet and get away with it—though some think this one did. It is a tale of secrecy and torment and of great disproportionate frugality within a household of commanding means, along with great accumulated wealth, coupled with intense hatred and a simple desire for money. At least that is what most believed. But was it?

The Bordens were a family undermined by dubious affections among a patronizing father, a hated stepmother, and their two Victorian daughters, living in a smoldering cauldron of mistrust and dissension. Lizzie and Emma Borden perceive their stepmother as an intruder and an unworthy heir to their father's fortune and affection, and prosecutor Hosea Knowlton is prepared to prove that it was Lizzie who killed her and her father.

Our story begins outside the courtroom in New Bedford, the country's leading whaling port. Euripides, fourth century, B.C., Greek tragedian and playwright, stands on the front steps wrestling with the complexities of law and justice. He questions his loyalties to Lizzie Borden and the damage she may inflict upon what little advances have been made by women throughout the ages. His is a heart ruled by tolerance, permissiveness, and compassion. He agonizes over Lizzie's possible culpability and the implications it may have on his life's work and the heroines he has written so passionately about. Euripides stands by Lizzie with compelling optimism and generous clemency. But he suffers with a mind plagued by suspicion and mistrust, of the accused and her deeds. He finds similarities between the character of Lizzie Borden and the heroines he has written about. All of them are strong, stubborn, and confident; he has preferred writing about them as forceful. To him, Lizzie is a mere mortal, no different than any other lady of her time, with all of the graceful attributes and shortcomings, but in Lizzie's case, more corporeal than most. As the case unfolds, Euripides continues to feverishly defend the integrity of Lizzie, along with the honor and glory that is womanhood.

While Euripides lectures the crowd outside, inside the courthouse Clarence Darrow, famous American attorney and civil libertarian, accompanies one William Jennings Bryan, lawyer, statesman, and a devout Presbyterian, in taking a harsher and more pragmatic view of Lizzie Borden and jurisprudence. For both men, guilt and innocence are subjective matters. Euripides, is ruled by the heart, but to men of law, bleeding sentiment has no place in the contest of litigation. Typical of their profession, both Darrow and Bryan are ruled by the mind. Defending the merits of good and evil, of innocence or guilt—these are procedural matters. The defense of their cause is the only true end to a means. If falsehood supports truth then guilt must walk free. Rewards are measured on a monetary scale, with justice a battle of wits by masters of syntax. To them, the legal campaign for the truth in the Borden case should be nothing more than an exercise in semantics—a tourney of competency, a contest to match wit and skill. But it is more. Fresh from the Scopes trial in Tennessee, both men have been inflicted with a sense of principle and ethics.

William Jennings Bryan—an advocate for deity and the purity of mankind—had always preordained Lizzie Borden to be unquestionably guilty. Darrow, sorry for beating up on his associate, who he battered on the stand at the Scopes trial, convinces Bryan that they should go back in time and try the Borden case again, giving William Jennings Bryan a chance to overturn history. In doing so, he challenges William Jennings Bryan to a game of poker to decide guilt or innocence—whether Lizzie goes free or hangs.

Bryan, who despises Darrow's agnostic doctrine, takes this case personally. And though his religious belief considers card play the game of demons, he decides that he will use the devil's own game against him, and agrees to Darrow's offer of a game of poker to decide Lizzie's fate. Thus law and all that is good is granted another opportunity to make things right and find Lizzie Borden guilty. At least that is how Bryan sees it.

Therefore on this day, the 5th of June 1893, starts the trial of the century, the trial of Lizzie Andrew Borden, to be judged by her peers and God, or the outcome of a simple game of cards.

What is a father, but a lover of gauzy kisses
You have become a crystal hull lacking chine
a pitted jewel ruptured of pigment,
when for love you refuse canvas
pouring fidelity upon a stony shore
and spilling the abiding quietus of a daughter's craving.

In your lack of devotion and adoration
spoiled with imparting disregard
to the wretched begging of a child
you drop anchor in the void of complacency .

For neither riches nor your warmth have unfurled
but instead they have become a proxy in my bosom
where uneasy lies the heart.

Lizzie Borden

Cast of Characters

BAILIFF: The Bailiff swears witnesses in and makes announcements, including introducing the Judge. He appears effeminate in manner and dainty in walk. Most of the time he is bored and removed from the events around him.

THOMAS BARLOW and EVERETT BROWN: Two teenage boys, witnesses for the Defense. Street-wise kids who come across as honest.

ELI BENCE: Clerk from Smith's Pharmacy, and witness for the Prosecution. Eli is overwhelmed by his experience at the trial. He thinks highly of himself and that he is there to perform. (It should be noted that Eli Bence did not testify at the original trial.)

ANDREW BORDEN: Murder victim and Lizzie's father. He appears to Lizzie as an apparition for about a minute, or the time it takes Lizzie to recite the poem, "By the Naked Pear Tree." No speaking part.

EMMA BORDEN: Sister of Lizzie Borden. Not a speaking part.

LIZZIE BORDEN: 32, woman accused of chopping up her stepmother and father with a hatchet, in Fall River, Massachusetts, 1892. Lizzie is confident and somewhat removed from incidents in the courtroom until the skull of her father is presented. She feels unjustly accused. She is very affected by her past, but hopes for promise in her future, which is reflected in her poetry.

SEABURY BOWEN: Family doctor. Eccentric and fascinated by his profession.

WILLIAM JENNINGS BRYAN: Middle-aged. Austere, conservative, and religious. Former representative from the state of Nebraska, served as Secretary of State under Woodrow Wilson, and ran unsuccessfully for President three times. His legacy is channeled through his participation in the Scopes Monkey Trial of 1925. Like Darrow, Bryan can control who sees him and who does not.

ADELAIDE CHURCHILL: Middle-aged widow. Next door neighbor to the Bordens. She is gregarious and friendly. Her mind wanders at times to events in her life that have nothing to do with the trial, which annoys the prosecuting attorney.

CLARENCE DARROW: Middle-aged. Very liberal, opinionated, and probably the most intelligent person in the room. Often pretends he doesn't know what is going on. He is self-assured. Civil Libertarian made popular by the famous John Thomas Scopes Trial of 1925, better known as the Scopes Monkey Trial. Some people can see and hear Darrow, while others cannot. He controls who sees him and who does not.

DEMON: Demon woman's voice in poem, "Mrs. Churchill Please do Come."

DR. WILLIAM DOLAN: The prosecution's medical doctor. His testimony is direct and professional. There is nothing uncommon about him until the skull of Andrew Borden is displayed in court, at which time he goes out of character and performs like a magician.

EURIPIDES: Old man with white beard and white hair. His address and poetry is dynamic, authoritative, and compelling. Though he is hopeful for the acquittal of Lizzie Borden, he is suspicious of her and doesn't trust her innocence or the Court. He is worried that Lizzie will damage the reputation of women. He stands outside the courtroom where he lectures the public on the merits of his plays, and lobbies and supports the goodness that is womanhood.

OLD FISHERMAN: Middle-aged, fishing pole over his shoulder. Speaks in broken English. Possibly an immigrant common to the area.

JOHN FLEET: Assistant Marshal to police. Supercilious and nervous, he thinks he is in command but acts the fool.

ANDREW JENNINGS: Middle-aged. Tall and slender, he is Lizzie Borden's attorney. He sports a neatly-trimmed Victorian mustache. He is distinguished, often kind to the witnesses, and competent.

REV. JUBB: Elderly and austere looking. Jubb is Lizzie Borden's confidant and pastor. Not a speaking part.

JUROR: Though reference is made to twelve jurors, only the foreman is seen, along with twelve empty chairs. The juror must be male, according to history. Although his suit is neat and clean, it doesn't fit him very well—a sign that he is a common man and rarely dresses for such occasions.

HOSEA KNOWLTON: Middle-aged, bearded, and stout, Knowlton has somewhat of a Napoleonic complex and easily flies off the handle. The Commonwealth's leading prosecutor.

HYMAN LUBINSKY: Early 20s. Lubinsky is gregarious, good-natured, and comes across as very honest. He has a deep Jewish and/or Russian accent. Think Brooklyn when it comes to an accent. Ice cream peddler, and witness for the defense.

JOHN MORSE: 60s. Mysterious, dismissive, but very sure of himself. Uncle of Lizzie Borden, witness for the prosecution.

PREGNANT MOTHER WITH CHILDREN: Her head is wrapped with a scarf, her clothing is neat and clean but somewhat ragged. She should have at least one child in her arms and two at her side.

MICHAEL MULLALY: Late 20s. Mullaly is Irish with a slight brogue. He is eager to be cooperative and his testimony appears sincere. One of the policemen sent to search the house on the day of the crime.

PARTICIPANTS IN COURTROOM: As many as the director feels are needed.

JUDGE, EDMUND LESTER PEARSON: Middle-aged. Pearson is authoritative and in control. He was the author best known for his 1937 book, *The Trial of Lizzie Borden*, stands in as Judge.

JULIAN RALPH: Young reporter for the *New York Sun*. He is overly excited about attending the trial of Lizzie Borden.

ALICE RUSSELL: 30s. Stern and proper, sad and lonely, but righteous. She is Lizzie and Emma Borden's best friend. She betrays friendship for justice.

BRIDGET SULLIVAN: 20s. Irish maid with thick brogue. Bridget is mousy and fearful, suspicious, and feels uncomfortable in her testimony. Worked as a maid for the Borden Family and was the only other person at home when Andrew and Abby Borden were killed. Reported to have seen nothing.

CROWD, NEWSPAPERMEN, SPECTATORS: As many as the director feels are needed.

Costumes

Most everyone is dressed according to their own historical period in time. CLARENCE DARROW and WILLIAM JENNINGS BRYAN are dressed with 1925 period clothing, Euripides is attired in 400 B.C. white robes and sandals, etc.

There are three characters who are dressed out of their period, with elaborate, ornate attire, and who perform out of character as well. This is to add a snippet of visual parody and satire to the play. They are the JUDGE, BAILIFF, and DOCTOR DOLAN. The dress is expressly chosen to lampoon the shortfalls of the legal and medical establishment of the time.

JUDGE: Dressed in a British eighteenth century robe. His attire is of a royal English judge, with white fur trimmings or possibly red robes, and sporting an official-looking medallion hanging from a gold chain around his neck.

BAILIFF: Cheerful fellow and very effeminate. His attire is tight and unconventional—a cross between someone in *West Side Story* and a magician's assistant. Somewhat flamboyant, he should be wearing a suit jacket, preferably a ceremonial one with long tails. Think Liberace.

DR. DOLAN: Dressed like a magician—all in black, white ruffled shirt, colorful cravat, top hat, and black cape with red lining. Under his cape is a long-tailed jacket similar to the one worn by the Bailiff but more formal.

WILLIAM JENNINGS BRYAN: Attire as would be worn by a political gentleman in 1925.

CLARENCE DARROW: Dressed in an off-white suit, dark tie, and straw hat. Against Bryan's neat attire, Darrow appears shabby.

LIZZIE BORDEN: Dressed in dark attire, black, or as was typical in most period newspaper illustrations (1893).

The costumes of everyone else not specifically described here should be period 1893.

Sets and Stage Scene

Inside courtroom

Sets and stage should be left up to the director, and should be as complex or as simple as the director sees fit. Whatever set is chosen, it should have suggestions, indicators, or a visual portrait and likeness of a late nineteenth century courthouse.

Inside there will be a small card table at the rear of the room, by the entrance doors, where a portrait of Abraham Lincoln hangs on the wall above it, and where CLARENCE DARROW and WILLIAM JENNINGS BRYAN spend most of their time playing poker and discussing the case.

When testifying, witnesses will stand behind a railing, which was common in 1893 in most courtrooms. The JUDGE will sit up high at his bench commanding the courtroom.

LAWYERS will have their own stations, tables, where they sit facing the bench with reporters and spectators behind them.

The JURY box will have twelve chairs, or less if the director so chooses, but only one JUROR. Being the JURY FOREMAN, he represents the other eleven, which are not present.

Outside courtroom

The courthouse exterior should display a stoop or veranda with steps, Roman or Greek architectural white Ionic columns, with a brick wall and front entrance behind them. Simple courthouse yard/street scenes, with CROWD standing around—again, the simplicity or complexity left up to the director.

Waterfront scene

The New Bedford water scene is of a whaling port, littered with stacks of wood, whale oil drums or casks, stacks of rope, anchors, etc. Stone or wooden docks overlook the bay forward and the rising city in the background. The sounds are of seagulls and surf. If possible, an image of a whale boat, boom sprit, with lines and masts, depict a working waterfront. Again, the complexity or simplicity of the scene should be left up to the director.

Lighting

Lighting is key here as it is constantly changing. Most, if not all, of LIZZIE BORDEN's poetry is recited in a darkened room, with the only artificial light upon her face and/or upper body. This focuses awareness on the poet and poem. This may also be true of the poem that is recited by BRIDGET SULLIVAN.

EURIPIDES and WILLIAM JENNINGS BRYAN's poetry is recited in natural daylight, since they occur outdoors. Lizzie's poetry recital is toward the climax of the play, when she is speaking to CLARENCE DARROW, and is in a darkened room, with illumination on LIZZIE BORDEN or CLARENCE DARROW, or both, as the director chooses.

Satire

Most of the parody and satire is included in the poetic testimony, with the exception of the scenes when the JUDGE enters the room, at which time the entire courtroom, including LIZZIE BORDEN, SPECTATORS, LAWYERS, and JURY, with the exception of CLARENCE DARROW and WILLIAM JENNING BRYAN, stand and break into cheers, whistles, and applause. This is the vital strand that adds a burlesque caricature to the play.

There is instructional narration throughout the written version of the play with descriptions of certain scenes, so as to communicate a visual portrayal and aid the production for readers.

By the Naked Pear Tree

ACT I
Scene One

Outside the courtroom, EURIPIDES stands, beckoning a CROWD OF SPECTATORS. His white robe, draped over his left shoulder, complements the huge, fluted white columns that hold up a slate roof over the stately building. He paces in and out of the columns in deep thought, as the onlookers walk over in curiosity.

He waits patiently as SPECTATORS stroll over to hear him speak. When he is ready, he marches down the courtroom steps and speaks in a loud, shouting voice.

EURIPIDES: Come near, come ear, all good people,
as we approach this time of heed
for women there now be plundered
leaving womanhood to bleed,
this is a virtuous varied time
an assault on all womankind
and a key to this mire we need.

For this Eve may degenerate us all,
be it wealthy or poor alike,
on this day, this humble town
goodness and evil ignite,
this fisherman's morning sun
this trial has now begun
and justice may well be smite.

FISHERMAN: *(In a rough Yankee accent.)*
And if guilty is her plea
what does this mean for us
what does this mean to me?

EURIPIDES: This may mean nothing to you,
               this betrayal of womanly trust,
               thus this hymn which she sings
               of the axe that she swings
               returning man back into dust.
               We look to the law
               the court of the land
               where administrators of justice
               to the crime that's at hand,
               and those who be ambitious
               the riches they command
               to discover the truth
               the killer of this woman
               the murderer of this man.

               Ride your ego of power and gold
               bear all the children that life dare hold,
               render our pangs and misgivings
               but relinquish your riches
               in exchange for our soul,
               and pander to Deity
               before you're too old
               and if your name be Borden
               lay not down your head
               clutch tight all your cards
               on sofa or bed
               hold to your money
               but be not profane
               as to leave a daughter
               bitter and lame.

               For this, my good public,
               you need not a seer
               to foretell what was coming
               to know what was near,
               life lacks compassion
               it exists without fear
               to exercise all insolence
               is to kiss not a tear.

FISHERMAN: A good man of counsel,
               you seem to appear
               in defense of the woman
               is what brings you here,

and what must we do
by the outcome we fear
can you tell or predict
what the Gods want made clear
can guilt truly blemish
are the blows so severe
to tarnish the name
and the esteem of Medea.

EURIPIDES bows his head, contemplating what was just said. He stretches out his arms and addresses the SPECTATORS.

EURIPIDES: My Helen, my Greece,
which I always portray
I arrive here today
to uncover the truth
in this bloody melee,
and from where I stand
where whaling began
justice may have its decay.

For you all know me well
with interest I write
of strong righteous heroines
and the men they entice,
in conflict and battle
and wars from the start
till virginity and chastity
takes a spear to the heart.

CLARENCE DARROW, who was listening among the SPECTATORS, steps forward and addresses EURIPIDES. Unlike the Greek, he does not recite poetry or verse when he speaks.

CLARENCE DARROW: I understand, Sir, that your virtues as a writer of story and verse are unparalleled. I have studied you in university. As a literary storyteller you have made your place in history. But, if I may plea—put aside your skill as playwright and let us act out the part of prophet, your Cassandra, your love of Troy. I know you would like me to defend Lizzie Borden, thus the heroines of your past. But what say you of the accused—the ramifications of her part in women's destiny, short term or long?

EURIPIDES paces, stroking his chin. He nods, squints, and smiles.

EURIPIDES: I can only say—
she cannot look back—at a melting sun
this steel horse sprints away with her
through thorny briers and life undone
a house of despair, to let evil stir.

Though all her Virgins have tumbled down
no savior comes to see her free
in an arid moon she will wear the gown
of steadfast resolve which will be her key.

She will not look back, a father's waning fire
she will ride the axe toward a mounting field
to climb the ridge towards her desire
beyond bloody cliffs where her heart can heel.

Though all her fences have fallen down
and her mind and heart refuse to speak
a cup of love will soon be found
she-will-not-blink, though life looks bleak.

And this steel horse she cannot stop
unlike Lot's wife she'll not look back
and of this hill she will reach the top
where her heart will change to white from black.

And from this steel horse she'll dismount
leave behind a blood stained past
where she's left, her dreams that she can't count
when they're set free, the sins she'll cast.

DARROW: I have no doubt, as you say, that she will put it all behind her. I dare add, she may even prevail. But being a man of God. What will she do with life? Will her friends stay loyal? And being a woman subject to the cloth, what will she tell her Maker?

EURIPIDES: The sun never glistens
upon fractured wings
ordained by God,
and a father's festering sin—
with shackles bestowed
to the serpent within.

Upon a sitting room sofa
or a guestroom floor
she will sever the bond
and stain her soul red
and in a gash of time
weave a new bed.

Breaching all restraints
with festering love
she will fashion new wings
deliberate and slow—
and with the freedom it brings
her Creator forgo.

DARROW: I'm afraid that perhaps you are right. God is nothing to some. Well my Macedonian friend, I must get inside and see what I can do for you—for womankind. Perhaps one day you will write about a new protagonist. A Victorian heroine.

The early day's sun washes the building's smooth Ionic columns snowy white. NEWSPAPERMEN walk up the courthouse steps, towards the front doors. In alarm, EURIPIDES steps forward and shouts out, extending his arm like an iron rod, and points to the NEWSPAPERMEN with a tone of scorn and disdain.

EURIPIDES: There they be!

EURIPIDES pauses, lowers his voice, and shakes his head in disgust. The NEWSPAPERMEN ignore him and continue walking.

EURIPIDES: Virtue is a riddle lacking justice in print
discernment and God
is shaded by man,
and judgment to come
will twist to fit
when guilt drips kindly from a judicial stand.

And the Globe pressman
slaps the steel
strikes hard the font upon the page,
spins the truth
how we should feel
deflects the scene
commands the stage.

His word in print
is meant to impeach
in naked daylight
like a fish lacking scales,
for the Sophist account
rides the back of a leach
and reeks as the tide

whilst he rakes his tale.

Enter the poet, snaps a twig
dips the splinter by the quill,
in bloody script he'll twist and dig
burrow deep the heart of the Gods will.

"Innocent, guiltless,"
the laureate recites
when truth and deceit walk the same aisle,
a daughter as feral still has her rights
when the accusers rhyme
spews hollow with bile.

And the Yellow Kid Trade
gives chase every year
christening this woman
without morals from the Gods,
while the murdered Bordens
set the public at fear
and daughters of mercy
bear a guilty façade.

Who will temper this yellow dog press
tutor the journo in years to be,
when columnist's font fails to confess
and embrace the verdict given Lizzie.

Enter the poet, snaps a twig
dips the splinter by the quill,
with parchment from Eden
with a leaf from the fig
cloaks the shame of this Eve's ill.

And like the Bard of Avon
in verse will find
unlike the Pressman
all fettered and bound,
compel us to think
with heart and mind
beneath the ink where God is not found.
And the *Globe* Pressman
slaps the steel
strikes hard the font upon the page,
while the poet issues

a gratis appeal
with passion, fury, fever, and rage,
with verse and rhyme
he strives to heal
this yellow print war
the Pressman has waged.

DARROW: *(Talking to himself.)* It's going to be a long, long day. *(He turns and begins to walk away.)*

EURIPIDES points over his head at the red brick courthouse.

EURIPIDES: Magistrate's advocate
with phallus and law
the feather of the wealthy
the anvil of the poor,
where the poet's dare tread
with verse they deplore
this colosseum of justice
we await at the door.

And with silver and gold
in defense of her sins
will scaffold her fall
whether she loses or wins,
with the color of money
unlike yours or I
of the hue of our skin
or the color of your eye
of impropriety and crime
would they dare let fly
if this woman be guilty
will transgression belie.

A PREGNANT MOTHER with CHILDREN hanging from her hand is disturbed by what she has heard and calls out to EURIPIDES.

PREGNANT MOTHER:
She is innocent, good Sir,
I stand in support
she be a lady of faith
and no crime of that sort
would be done by a sister
and guiltless she'll be found
by God and this court

to freedom she be bound,
for no fair spinster
would slaughter the calf
the milk which she suckles
with a life cut in half
no... I can not accept
that this woman is vile
they must be mistaken
she will prove it at trial.

EURIPIDES, unsure of the support that he lends LIZZIE BORDEN, shouts out in exasperation. He points to the street at the WOMAN's feet with an expression of repugnance. The PREGNANT WOMAN backs away.

EURIPIDES: In gutters spill the virtue
of motherly milk
thus up goes the curtain
of bengaline silk,
a crime done of woman
with axe in her hand
and penalties dishonored
will the public withstand
when God and Demon
both take the same stand.

This menses around us
we must wipe clean
to speak the unspoken
to punish the fiend,
in defense of all women
and the goodness of God
she must be found pure
of the truth which they prod,
and not stain the maidens
which history has not marred.

EURIPIDES watches just as CLARENCE DARROW enters the courthouse. With his arm pointing at the sky, he shouts so DARROW can hear him.

EURIPIDES: Thus I raise my quill
to exploit this transgression
strife upon woman
of puss and infection,
within madness and morality

of this sanguinary soul
we must crush the snake's head
and of justice uphold,
the poison and venom
we need to dissolve
among rabid serpents
this puzzle must solve,
between syphilis and virtue
upon each other will fold
we must not let them mate
what testimony will hold
this uncommon young lady
when the truth be all told.

Let salvation's bell ring
for those who attend
the trial of the century
to which we will lend
the crimes and the sins
of one Lizzie Borden.

BLACKOUT

ACT I
Scene Two

WILLIAM JENNINGS BRYAN and JULIAN RALPH are standing in the courtroom atrium. CLARENCE DARROW, straw hat in one hand, walking cane in the other, enters the space. As he approaches the two men, he points his bamboo cane at them in jest. BRYAN takes JULIAN RALPH by the elbow and walks over to greet him.

BRYAN: Mr. Ralph, I would like to introduce to you the most progressive defense attorney in the country today. Advocate for the underprivileged, downtrodden, and misunderstood—Clarence S. Darrow. Excuse the straw hat. Mr. Darrow is much more capable than he appears.

DARROW: The hat is a reminder that one must exercise leisure and not get carried away by one's work. It's also cool and stylish.

RALPH: (Leaning over, he offers his hand.) Pleasure is mine, Sir.

BRYAN: Mr. Darrow's interest in the case is strictly topical. He has agreed to sit in on the trial after being persuaded by a clandestine client he wishes to keep anonymous.

RALPH: Your client with the defense or prosecution, Mr. Darrow.

DARROW: No, no, it is just a favor for a friend, someone I have always admired greatly, a writer of plays, you could say. He's not a client at all. Just a Greek.

RALPH: But you share the same interest and outcome.

DARROW: That's safe to say.

RALPH: Very admirable to come all this way for a friend. Ah, how far did you say you traveled, Mr. Darrow?

DARROW: Did I say? Can't recall mentioning it.

BRYAN: Well, let us go on the record and state that we traveled more a journey of space and time than miles.

RALPH: Space and time?

DARROW: All I can say is it felt like it took over 30 years to get here. Still, I feel younger than ever.

DARROW and BRYAN break into laughter. RALPH chuckles, not quite sure what to make of the reply, or what was so funny.

DARROW: So you are a venerable member of the press, Mr. Ralph.

RALPH: New York Sun, Sir.

DARROW: Well, prepare yourself. This has been classified as the crime of the century. Landmark judicious decrees will abound in this case. You will have plenty to write about.

RALPH: Yes, Sir. I'm certain.

DARROW: *(Throws his spent cigarette to the floor and steps on it.)* Then again it could all be dull as hell.

BRYAN clears his throat and solicits the men's attention before RALPH has a chance to inquire.

BRYAN: Gentlemen, shall we get going? Proceedings will be starting soon. Those early to the theatre get the best seats.

DARROW: Did you not make reservations, my good man?

BRYAN: That I did, that I did. I have set up a small card table at the rear of the courtroom. Everyone will be out of our way there, and we will have an excellent view of activities.

DARROW: Shall we go in, gentlemen?

BLACKOUT

ACT I
Scene Three

DARROW, RALPH, AND BRYAN walk through a set of large, swinging, mahogany, glass doors leading into the courtroom chamber. The court BAILIFF walks in and lifts some window shades to let more light into the room. BRYAN sits down at the small table, his back to the rear wall, at the back of the courtroom. He looks over some notes. DARROW sits facing him and the swinging doors which are just off to his left. He pulls out a pack of cigarettes and lights one. He studies the reflection in the door glass of participants behind him as they fill the courtroom. At the same time DARROW can scrutinize activities in the foyer outside the room. JULIAN RALPH stands by the table with bemused curiosity, befuddled by his two companions' behavior.

Just then, LIZZIE BORDEN enters the courtroom by a side entrance. She is accompanied by her Attorney, ANDREW JACKSON JENNINGS, the REVEREND JUBB, and her sister, EMMA. LIZZIE breaks away from her private entourage, walks over to a window, and looks out to the street. EURIPIDES, who stands just outside in the middle of the road, bows to her. LIZZIE ignores him as he points up to her and continues his poetic litany. So loud is his voice that most in the courtroom can hear him.

EURIPIDES: Pregnant with justice
she shines her image upon the court
for family, for friend, for foe… for God.

She asks not or adjure their support
and parades quietly
in poise of vigor and pride.

In Hades she has fused
a bond, an alliance
and to her Maker
she pleads nothing to hide.

Look down upon the broken and dead
by the iron brought down on his face
and the loathing that crushed her head
rancid love in blood she must taste.

So wag your fist to your Lord in the sky
her future is written within a cloud
while the dead can't chant, the living will lie
she'll wear her defiance as a blessed shroud.

And stand aside who dare throw stones
let innocence trowel a sacred path
with the rendered flesh and shattered bone
with the demons with whom she dined and sat.

And payment she painfully extracted
with the sins of all womankind
she'll kiss aside the law she fractured
while the bells of God do chime.

BRYAN taps the back of DARROW's hand, and points out LIZZIE BORDEN. Without turning around, DARROW looks up at the mahogany doors and scrutinizes her reflection in the glass, which is superimposed over HOSEA KNOWLTON's image as he enters from the foyer.

LIZZIE appears forlorn and in deep thought as she stares out the window. Suddenly the light in the courtroom fades as the light on her face brightens. The voices and sounds of the room grow silent. With no one watching, she stares out the window and dries a tear from her cheek with a pink lace handkerchief, and begins to recite.

LIZZIE: I watched tears of fruit
Swing by the skin
How easy life ends
With no forgiveness of sin
Ripe without pigment
With life's sweetness shaved thin.

I took my seat by the barn
My back rubbed the wall
Bleeding chips of red paint
On my shoulders they fall
With a fury and wrath
I can no longer forestall.

Pears tumbled to earth
And peppered the ground
Nineteen I did count
With laughter well found

While she fell on her face
Without making a sound.

On a hot August day
I waxed with disdain
Awaiting the scythe
Where ten pears remained
To rot on the vine
With my anguish and pain.

In a covet for life
I wish them to pay
Thus, pear after pear
Dropped where they lay
I brushed clean my shoulders
The last pear fell away
And by the naked pear tree
I no longer need stay.

A light shines upon the JUROR, then fades back into darkness. LIZZIE is startled by it. These are the twelve souls who can damn her behind bars for the rest of her adult life. (For production simplicity, the jury is made up of one man and eleven empty chairs.) LIZZIE recites.

LIZZIE: The jail
                 that jail.

                 I will dress myself in steel bars
                 bars placed around me
                 black, black as the hearts
                 of those who know the truth
                 where I have been kept
                 these many months.

                 Bastille far from Swansea
                 the jury will undress
                 and tarnish my plea
                 of my freedom divest—
                 or perhaps let me go
                 when my chastity I confess
                 but I will never concede
                 or fall to my knee.
                 Outside the cool summer rain
                 washes the soot from the street
                 in a warm winter heart

can it cleanse or secrete
the innocence I declare
in victory or defeat.

Alone—
no one can witness as I make love
to the solid cold barricade
which tempers the marrow in my soul
not unlike the craving
or desire to return
to that unspeakable place
where the blood did spill
not quite in the slum
but far from the hill.

I will take comfort in my hold
where my dreams have all aged
like a tigress I'll cry
as a lioness I rage.

And my tears will not rust
those bars that contain
or would I allow them to thwart
or the floor to stain
against all my zeal
to assume this iron
embrace this steel
allow defeat not to rein
or my ambitions to steal
a jail
a jail
I will never revel.

The light in the room slowly returns to normal. The REVEREND JUBB walks over and takes LIZZIE by the arm, escorting her to her seat. The scene returns to DARROW and BRYAN at the rear of the courtroom. BRYAN scouts the room carefully.

BRYAN: I don't see the defendant.

RALPH: There, you see—being seated by the Reverend. The older woman to her left—I think that is the sister, Emma.

BRYAN: Oh yes, yes... that is Lizzie Borden! Not the heinous fiend most make her out to be. Even in refined attire she looks... well, smart. Ink blue feathered straw hat—common. Not a cultivated head dress for formal use... but she wears it well.

DARROW: *(He chuckles.)* A critic of fashion, are we, Bryan?

DARROW turns in his chair and steals a glance LIZZIE's way. He removes his straw hat from his lap and flings it onto the table.

DARROW: You see gentlemen, straw is more popular than ever. It is the fiber, the thread that weaves the classes. If it's fair for the beau monde and Lizzie Borden it's all right for me.

RALPH: Finally! Lizzie Borden. There sits the most infamous woman who ever lived. My, my—she appears very ladylike, almost gentle. I dare add, modest even.

DARROW chuckles and sneers.

DARROW: What did you expect—Medusa? Look at her. She commands absolute mastery of herself. An attorney could not wish for a more exemplary client. Polished, unassuming, yet composed and poised. She makes her sensations and emotions inconspicuous and enigmatic to an impertinent public, most of whom know she is innocent but believe she is guilty.

BRYAN: If I am to subscribe to your sentiment, Clarence, she is the most injured of innocents or the blackest of monsters.

RALPH: She either hacked her father and stepmother to pieces with the furious brutality of the ogre in Poe's story of the Rue Morgue, or some other person did it, and she suffers the double torture of losing her parents and being wrongfully accused of their murders.

DARROW: Now, now, gentlemen. Have some compassion. At the very least, try to exercise some objectivity. Don't kill and eat the chicken before it grows feathers. I am aware that I am the elementary pupil here when it comes to particulars about this case. The mind is not as sharp as it once was, and reflecting back to my days at academia, I remember very little, but...

BRYAN: I come as a very prepared counselor, and I intend to see justice served. Though she appears angelic to you, gentlemen, I am convinced she contains the devil himself in her heart.

DARROW: You must excuse my colleague, Mr. Ralph; you see, I believe in the benevolence of mankind, of womankind, that one is innocent before proven otherwise. Now Mr. Bryan, here, on the other hand, has come prepared to condemn the defendant with his righteous orthodoxy. He is after all the true Nazarene among us.

BRYAN: I assure you, she is guilty—guilty as sin. Those murders were a transgression upon God and all mankind.

DARROW: And what of womankind?

BRYAN: You know my meaning, Clarence.

DARROW: So, let me understand. You volunteer a pre-trial conviction before listening to the facts. Very sectarian for a political cleric, Bryan, would you not agree?

BRYAN: No, I would not. All I am doing is playing the devil's advocate for the prosecution, that is all. Besides, you and I know the story over the years, we have read all the papers.

DARROW: So, we are counsel for the devil, are we now? I thought we agreed to ignore all we know and read and start anew?

BRYAN: There you go with the devil. I thought we were not to bring religion into this case. Was that not one of my contentions before agreeing to come?

DARROW: *(Winks at RALPH.)* You're the one who placed God on the stand.

BRYAN: Aah!

DARROW: Are you a man of God, Mr. Ralph?

RALPH: If accused of murder and placed at the stand anyone would subscribe to the Almighty, would you not say?

DARROW: *(Chuckling.)* I suppose you're right, young man.

BRYAN: Mr. Darrow's a skeptic at heart, you see. He is not a believer of anything he can't see, hear, smell, taste, or feel.

DARROW: Not completely true. I believe in the rights of the citizen and in his or her pursuit of happiness, whether rich, poor, black, or white. And in my experience I have discovered it is the poor which are in need of my services most. Therefore, to the senses Mr. Bryan just mentioned, I add the most vital one when assessing human character—the heart.

RALPH: Is that true, Mr. Darrow?

DARROW: Is what true?

RALPH: You are not a man of God?

DARROW: If I shatter your illusions, Mr. Ralph, you have my heartfelt apology, but I do not believe in God because I do not believe in Mother Goose.

BRYAN: Blasphemous, Clarence, blasphemous. The man has asked a worthy question. Why do you ridicule his convictions?

DARROW: A worthy question, indeed. But the gentleman never expressed his convictions one way or the other. So, I don't see how you translate my remark as ridicule.

BRYAN: I resent that! With all good intentions to Mr. Ralph, he is not the only other gentleman present.

DARROW looks over to RALPH, leans in with a determined squint.

DARROW: I am an agnostic, Mr. Ralph. My apology if I do not pretend to know what many ignorant men are sure of. Belief in the Almighty does not make man righteous, noble and decent. I have arrived at my conclusions by using not only my mind but my heart. You may hold me to that one. But there is more evil in the hearts of men than in their brains. So as you can see, the heart is the most vital of senses. Sadly, most men have no sense at all—not even the common variety.

RALPH: *(Writing in his notepad.)* What is our rebuttal, Mr. Bryan?

BRYAN: Mr. Darrow speaks of the heart, when he really means his wallet.

DARROW: Not so. I'm certain that Mr. Bryan will tell you that money is the root of all evil. But some of us see life differently. I say money is not the root, it is the flower. The root is deep in the heart of man.

BRYAN: Mr. Ralph, Mr. Ralph, put it away. Save your note-taking for the trial. We are here as observers—not litigants. A friend does not take notes on a friend.

RALPH: *(Sheepishly puts down his pad.)* Sorry, force of habit, you know.

BRYAN: Now, Clarence, if you are such a defender of the poor and the subjugated, why are you here in the defense of such a rich defendant such as Lizzie Borden, a privileged woman whose family has multiplied their fortune off the backs of hard working poor, as you would put it?

RALPH: She is believed to be worth almost a million, is she not?

BRYAN: *(Leans over to DARROW.)* You heard what the man said. And may I add that no one can earn a million dollars honestly.

DARROW: My pursuit is not a monetary one. It is one based on principle. I am not here in support of the prosecution or the defense. As I have mentioned earlier, a Greek has championed me to be witness to justice, and to what he sees as the moral repute of womanhood. He is willing to let the cards fall where they may. And may I add that justice should have no monetary value. It should have nothing to do with how affluent or destitute one may be. But that is another story—an injustice all in itself.

RALPH: You keep mentioning this Greek?

BRYAN: Mr. Ralph, Clarence Darrow speaks in riddles. It is a defense he employs when he lacks a constructive response. It's a ploy towards deception. What else do you expect from a man who has no belief in the Almighty?

DARROW: Ah, Mr. Bryan, such a Scopian allegation to articulate. Takes a brave monkey to trumpet such accusations.

BAILIFF: Everyone please stand
              The proceeding has begun
              The honorable justice
              Edmund Lester Pearson.

JUDGE EDMUND LESTER PEARSON enters the court. The room breaks into pandemonium as the SPECTATORS jump to their feet and begin to applaud, whistle, and cheer for the start of the trial of the century. The JUDGE seats himself and immediately pounds the gavel. The room falls silent.

JUDGE: Let us begin
                 come to order please
                 you, Sir, in the back of the room
                 keep our voice at ease
                 silent now, silent
                 this din must all cease
                 if you please
                 if you please.

RALPH: *(Whispering.)* Well, gentlemen, you heard the judge.
BRYAN: You best get nearer the bench, Mr. Ralph, before all the prime
    stations are occupied.
DARROW: Yes, hurry young man, there... a chair right behind the defendant.
    Best seize it before it's gone.

*CLARENCE DARROW reaches into his pocket and pulls out a deck of playing
cards. RALPH glares at him in bemused cynicism. DARROW slams the deck
onto the table, making certain that his companion notices that the box is
sealed. Opening the carton he bangs them on the table several times to
square the deck, sending a resounding, booming echo throughout the room.
Simultaneously, the JUDGE does the same with his gavel.*

DARROW: Straight poker, Bryan, is that right?
BRYAN: Is there any other kind? What will we use for currency?
DARROW pulls out two boxes of matchsticks and flings one across the table.
DARROW: There's 200 matchsticks in each box. Each equal a dollar.
BRYAN opens the box and sticks a match in his mouth. It rests on his lip as
    he tumbles it across his mouth.
DARROW: Remember the rules?
BRYAN: Foible knowledge acquired in youth is rarely forgotten.
RALPH: Shh! Gentlemen, please. I implore you. Lower your voices. The
    court's come to order.
BRYAN: You're the participant here, Mr. Ralph. History summons you, not
    us. We are but mere observers. The judge speaks to you. The court can
    neither see us nor hear us, if that is what we wish.
DARROW: Yes, my boy. Bryan is correct. *(DARROW jumps to his feet waving
    his finger. The match bounces on his lower lip. He shouts to the bench.)*
    Carry on, Your Honor, you are not disturbing us.

*The JUDGE ignores him since he does not hear him. No one hears him but
RALPH. For as BRYAN has proclaimed, no one can hear or see them unless
they allow it. RALPH is stunned, unable to understand what is going on.*

BRYAN: There, you see, Mr. Ralph. We are not even present. Now go to
    work. Do your job. The New York Sun awaits you.

RALPH backs away, stumbling against a chair. He looks at DARROW and BRYAN as if he were seeing an apparition, as the two lawyers fade and disappear before his eyes. Quickly he scurries down the aisle to the front of the crowded courtroom where he is lost among the SPECTATORS.

DARROW: *(Nodding his head.)* Green with enterprise.

BRYAN: Oh I don't know. The boy's got moxie.

DARROW: Humph! Moxie is a term I would reserve for the defendant.

BRYAN: If you ask me she should be wearing the letter "A".

DARROW: Hawthorne would have made it the letter "M".

BRYAN: "M"?

DARROW: Murder. *(He deals the playing cards.)* Now what are the stakes?

BRYAN: The Uncle. One, John Vinnicum Morse. He will be the first wager.

DARROW: Mr. John Morse? Is that Scottish?

BRYAN: Old English stock, Clarence. You should know that.

DARROW: From what I read, he thinks he should be receiving restitution for his testimony.

BRYAN: Well, all that is significant to me is that he helps hang Lizzie Borden.

DARROW: Whether she hangs or is set free, my friend, may be determined by a pair of kings or a full house.

CURTAIN

ACT II
Scene One

*CLARENCE DARROW spreads the playing cards in his hand
and examines them. On the wall, above the head of WILLIAM
JENNINGS BRYAN, and tilting somewhat forward, hangs a
steel engraved portrait of Abraham Lincoln. In the glass
that protects the image, DARROW can clearly see the cards
that BRYAN holds.*

JUDGE: Jurors have been sworn
the plea has been said
the defendant has been warned
that her father is dead,

this court is now ready
to discover the truth
counselors make ready
to apply your dispute,

please present your case—
gentlemen take the floor
Mr. Jennings, if you may
to you we implore
to execute your plan,

and you, Mr. Knowlton
the case in your hand
and to your first witness
prepare for the stand
opening statements will commence
God bless this court
God bless this land.
Mr. Knowlton, are you primed

opening affirmations prepared
you may start at your leisure
with the witnesses you have snared.

*HOSEA KNOWLTON, attorney for the prosecution, with hands gripping his
lapels, studies the tips of his shoes as he walks in the direction of the JURY. He
pauses in reflection.*

KNOWLTON: Upon the fourth of August
of eighteen ninety two
a husband and his good wife
in crime we can't undo
were murdered in the light of day
after a meal of mutton stew.

Now—
it is not my purpose to weary you
with evidence or minor detail
or recite a sermon of woe and despair
prosecution we have here can't fail
for unlawful human agency
are intention we'll help unveil.

The prisoner who sits in the court
and lives on Second Street
short distance from the city hall
where one can live discreet
with sister, father, mother, maid
a railroad flat en suite.

You see the suspect dressed in black
the one with the haunting stare
the court will prove that she's the fiend
to chauffeur a town in despair
an old man, and old woman she did kill
their life she didn't care.

The poison she did try to buy
testimony will set the mood
for use to clean a seal skin cape
she's more than mean, she's shrewd
and of talk of poison in the milk
the druggist she can't elude
prussic acid she can't deny
though defense will disapprove.

And of a note delivered
as a diversion from the scent
like the hint she gave the maid
an eight cent sale event
she did not want them all to know
mother lay void and spent.

Mr. Foreman,
members of the jury,
do not become misled
with the axe, the dress, the blood
the circumstantial light we shed.

I'm sure you can read between the lines
and the chronicle which she has fed
of the dressing attire that she did burn
and the rifts in the victims' head.

Words that leap unto my lips
to the litigant we must inquire
Miss Lizzie where were you that day
how did you plan, scheme and conspire
Miss Borden do tell us the facts and the truth
for we'll prove that you are a liar
when this court is done dear girl
to jail you will retire.

Now—
listen closely, gentlemen,
the jury must understand
Lizzie Borden had a hate
for the wife of this old man
"she is a mean thing," she once said
and that's how it began
"she's not my mother, get that straight
I hate her when I can."

And in that house, behind closed doors
where bars and bolts and locks
and in those rooms were no privacy
not unlike a tinderbox
where the summer heat did bare down
Miss Lizzie waited like a fox
to prove the woman and the beast
a flawless case in paradox.

We will show that Lizzie lied
about where she was that day
in the barn or in the loft
and how long she did stay
in her room or in the yard
or where her stepmother lay
or standing abaft her father
she was sure to make him pay.

Gentlemen of the jury, please
this court without a doubt
will prove to you who did the deed
what this murder was all about
and with the evidence I decree
which carries a mass of clout
we will prove Miss Lizzie Borden
the brute who did strike out.

For the people of this fair state
we will save the soul of day
after all the truths are dealt
this assassin will be put away
when her alibi starts to dissolve
in this murderous dark ballet
for the hand she has unfairly dealt
justice will not delay.

To this humble court and bench I add
it's all I have to say.

JUDGE: Very well counselor,
of butchers and of sorrow
God bless this state
God bless this court
today, next week, tomorrow
We will have a fifteen minute break
Bailiff...

The JUDGE raps his gavel once and leaves. The BAILIFF walks forward and addresses the SPECTATORS to stand. As he walks he does so with swishy, proud little steps, shifting his weight from one leg to the other, his arms hanging limply by his side. The lights in the courtroom fade to dark. A low hum of voices fade in the blackness, as some SPECTATORS leave the courtroom and the hollow din goes silent. A solitary light shines upon LIZZIE, who is now standing, her arms resting on the railing before her—looking up at the ceiling as if up to heaven.

LIZZIE: I weary of this attire
of leaden black and blue
strangling my desire
in a reoccurring hue
with this Bedford cord life
I need to renew.

Life has turned stale
n' a swamp of tears
n' a fungus of rage
that dampens my fears
cold hard steel bars
hacking away the years.

Of poison and milk
of mutton in heat
in China blue silk
with the shattering
of teeth.

A Bedford cord, red
and Father's squab wife
by the side of the bed
an end to a life
is it justice well fed.

By a stranger in wait
of betrayal and hate
who stoke the fire
of this terrible fate.

And the bile in my heart
from my head to my feet
tears me apart
on that Second house Street,
that vile railroad flat
that fortress of sheep.

From this bengaline life
I need to escape
Father's philistine rules
this emotional rape

an unraveling spool
of appeal and plea
to live on the hill
where I ought to be
leaves nothing for me
to be free
to be free.

(Pause.)

Oh how I wish to be away from here,
someone take me away from here.

Emma, sweet Emma,
you were the concierge
to my shedding soul
take me away
take me
Emma—

Take me fishing
by the black waters of the Quequechan
with the grey river flow
the lines we will throw
to the fish from the land.

We will build us a raft
some sheets for a sail
behind old Slade Mill
I will gather and fill
bait, worms in a pail.

Emma, please take me away
from this house we will steal
where our passion can sway
my poor heart may heal
by the sea, by the bay.
To sleep in the sand
with cattails for a bed
where the sun can tan
and be happy and red
from Abby we'll stray
from the mutton she fed
we can both run away
from Father and dread.

Emma, take me fishing
by the tracks and the rail
I'll go to the barn
and to the loft I will scale
find me some iron
my pole and some twine
we will hook us a whale
lose this horror in time
Emma take me fishing...
please.

(Pause.)

I did love Father... I did. I remember how I treasured riding about town
with you. I would always beg, beg you to take me for a buggy ride. I
would sing...

Take me for a buggy ride
Father will you please
by my side we will go
to the Croft among the trees
where the tall maples grow
and my heart is on its knees.

Take me for a buggy ride
Mother will not go
and chase away the morning dew
to where the warm winds blow
where passion runs tried and true
and tears, cold, never flow.

Take me for a buggy ride
Emma will you please
to the throne where we belong
where our fancies all run free
the streets are wide, mansions strong
with the glimpse of the distant sea.

Take me for a buggy ride
before it's all too late
before the August summer kill
away from the house of hate
to my topaz upon the hill
before I lose my soul and faith.

Take me for a buggy ride
take me will you please
where the tall maples grow
to the Croft among the trees
take me for a buggy ride
a buggy ride...
please.

(Pause.)

If only you did, Father. Perhaps you and I would have lived forever. But, no....
no, it was not to be. I am left with that terrible day when I discovered
you.... dead. Yes dead. I remember calling out for Maggie the maid, to
Mrs. Churchill—"Mrs. Churchill, please do come," I said.

(Pause.)

Mrs. Churchill, please do come
someone has killed father...

DEMON: He quivers like a bow
              in the morgue sitting room
              life's leaving him real slow
              upon a horsehair tomb.

LIZZIE: Dr. Bowen, please do come
              though I fear there's no need...

DEMON: Afraid she is dead
              what a dastardly deed
              a blow to the head
              leaving her to bleed.

LIZZIE: Maggie down, please do come
              the windows were such a chore...

DEMON: Killers are all about
              have you locked the screen door
              heard not a moan or a shout
              what's that thump upon the floor.

LIZZIE: Miss Russell, please do come
              some coffee, or tea instead...

DEMON: Just burning this old dress
              that's been soiled, painted red

	from a chop I may confess
	that rendered them both dead.

LIZZIE: Emma please do come
            our whims we will fulfill...

DEMON: Do return without delay
            since they both are laying still
            all our ashes have bled away
            now we both can have our will.

LIZZIE lowers her head and rests it in her hand, in a desperate endeavor to stem the DEMON's voice inside her. She shouts...

LIZZIE: Get away all you demons!
            get away,
            get away,
            get away!

LIZZIE looks up and listens intently. Nothing. The room is silent.

LIZZIE: I remember laying there in that infertile bed, day after night, night after day, staring up at that fractured ceiling—no prospects, no promise, no hope— a long empty existence.

            After an age, a life of missed fortune
            missed adventure
            missed love,
            I lay on this hard stabbing bed
            staring up, curling chips,
            cracks on the ceiling above
            fractures like tainted rivers
            on a wrinkled torn chart
            taking me downstream
            into a valley of empty desire,
            chips like dry peeling skin
            bits and pieces of my mind
            flaking off,
            parched ambitions
            waiting in this Second Street bedroom
            waning into another desolate night
            illuminated by the dim orange glow
            of a smoky lantern giving no design
            to the upcoming day or life.

Just more of the same
from he who is crippled
tamed by sightless accord
perhaps by age
with she who I will not call mother.

And her,
she,
a sister, content
to advance no more,
pleased to just be
merely a daughter
left to wallow in the spinning current
to flounder, stumble
with social tides,
to be soulless
for I will not,
and I need not
any longer.

The light in the room returns to normal. The BAILIFF orders the SPECTATORS to stand. When the JUDGE walks in the SPECTATORS jump up and applaud, cheer, and whistle, some even stamping their feet. With a gleeful smile, the JUDGE puts up his hands to quiet the room as he sits. LIZZIE sits back down. The room goes silent.

Defense attorney's ANDREW JENNINGS prepares for his opening statement. JENNINGS paces the floor by the bench and the JURY, assessing his approach. He quietly hums "The Battle Cry of Freedom" under his breath, the famous American Civil War song of Union rally. He holds his arm up and sways a single finger with the cadence of the tune, as if conducting an invisible orchestra. He smiles to the JURY beckoning their approval.

JENNINGS: Catchy tune, would you not say, gentlemen?
              Let us begin.

              May it please Your Honor,
              Mr. Foreman, and Jury,
              we will prove to this court
              without doubt or mistrust
              Lizzie Borden is innocent
              of all this fury
              and the death of her parents
              on the fourth of August.

One of the victims
of this dastardly deed
was a client and friend
to many of you here,
for many of us now
I must warn you to heed
my client be innocent
it will prove very clear.

JENNINGS pauses, wags his finger, and hums the "Battle Cry" tune once more.

JENNINGS: Sorry, gentlemen. Can't seem to get that tune out of my head. Such a fancy ditty. Suits the purpose. Don't you think?

JUDGE: *(With reprimand.)* Mr. Jennings!

JENNINGS: *(Clears his throat.)* Ah yes, as I was remarking...

I may manifest more passion
than you think I should
the counsel does not cease
to become a man,
he wears neither cloak
or hangman's hood
when he becomes a servant
one does not join the Klan.

Fact and fiction have furnished
many examples of crime
have shocked the spirit
of reason and mind,
and the brutal character
of wounds you will find
my client did not deliver
whether nineteen or nine.

The accused is a young lady
thirty-two years of age
unblemished in character
her reputation is commanding,
we shall show this pure woman
led an honorable life
a member in the church
a maid in good standing.

As in the drama of Desdemona
in this judicial performance
she stands well within
the circle of presumption,
for I be the Othello
who protects this fair ward
until a reasonable doubt
is this jury's assumption.

Mr. Foreman and gentlemen,
there are two kinds of evidence
circumstantial and direct
of that you may claim,
now of the direct variety
the state is in lacking
with no blood, no weapon
they have no one to blame.

If you must throw aside
every fact which you have
any reasonable doubt
or fail to make fit,
like the bengaline silk
or a blood-covered axe
you are left with no choice
but to free, clear... acquit.
We shall show in addition
there were strangers around
Lizzie's visit to the barn
that she had gone inside,
about the police
their trip to the loft
their imagination alone
we can prove they have lied.

As to the burning of a dress
the one covered with paint
Alice Russell will testify
that Lizzie had declared,
the dress was well soiled
she burnt in daylight
with police all abound
and no cause to be scared.

And so, Mr. Foreman
gentlemen of the jury,
we present our case
of which you must uncover,
with reasonable doubt
of killing those folks
are the results you must find
with the facts you discover.

Incredulity is a posture
the state has embraced
that this Victorian damsel
they refuse to believe,
of impeachable conduct
she had dispatch
and with brawn or muscle
this murder she'd weave.

For we will uncloak
the proceedings against
by barristers to crime
who think they've unveiled,
the killer of ancients
of goodness and truth
the robber to life
of proportion and scale.
But you must remember
the traces to blood
foundation in trial
with weapon and proof,
you will not discover
implements of horror
in her purse or her hand
or in basement to roof.

And before I conclude
allow me to add—

JENNINGS begins to sing...

We'll rally round the spinster, boys,
we will rally once again.
Shouting the battle the cry of freedom,
we will rally from the hillside,
we will gather from the plain.

Shouting the battle cry of freedom,
we will welcome to our numbers the loyal and true,
the brave shouting
the battle cry of freedom...

The JUDGE pounds his gavel assertively.

JUDGE: Mr. Jennings, Mr. Jennings,
            stick to the statement at hand.
            This is not a stage for monkeys or ponies—
            do you understand?

JENNINGS: Sorry, Your Honor,
            got swept away
            I'm done with my statement
            I yield, I pray.

JUDGE: Mr. Knowlton, are you ready
            your case to install
            the indictment and burden
            to prove to us all
            the defendant is guilty,
            errant, and gall
            summon your first witness
            drop the cards where they fall.

KNOWLTON: I hail to the stand
            my first witness today
            one Mr. Morse
            with consent if I may
            from the court to my lips
            the testimony we'll weigh
            come forward to the stand
            without dally or delay.

*JOHN VINNICUM MORSE lumbers up to the stand looking nervous but smug.
He is a tall man and one who appears to be growing out of his clothes, which
are wrinkled and drab.*

Direct Examination.

KNOWLTON: Mr. Morse, state your age
            tell us where you reside
            and about August the fourth
            any secrets you may hide.

MORSE: If it may please the court
            I think I'm 60 in age,
            I live n' Dartmouth by the sea
            where I earn a modest wage.

KNOWLTON: Mr. horse tender Morse,
            Now—
            you be the brother-in-law
            who napped in the bed
            by the shock and the gore,
            your perchance Weybosset trip
            perhaps you care to draw
            of the food that was served
            to the blood upon the floor.

MORSE: I can only declare of being afraid
            taking blame for the crime
            if I loitered, if I stayed,
            so a flight to Weybosset
            was a journey I did braid
            n' that jaunt I did take
            'tis a visit well paid,
            to my niece and my nephew
            several hours I did stay
            while the axe wildly dropped
            in sanguinary glum foray.

KNOWLTON: Are you trying to allege
            you were not really there
            when she shaved Borden's face
            and parted Abby's hair,

            are we to acquiesce
            you did not have a nose
            who committed the crime
            who delivered the blows,

            and when it all happened
            are you truly that slow
            or is it a lack of wit
            these facts you don't know?

MORSE: If you please, dear Sir,
            you must understand
            of this dastardly crime

I lack motive or plan.

I'm a traveler, a drifter
with no ties or bosses
just a dude in the business
of peddling horses.

KNOWLTON: Tell us of your flight
the moment you return
the events of that day
any evidence of concern.

MORSE: I arrived close to noon
must admit with a scare
pretended to be a stranger
went out back for a pear.

KNOWLTON: You were careful and hungry
that we will assume
now, did you emerge
and can we all presume,
you entered the house
you entered the room?

MORSE: I walked up the back porch
Mr. Sawyer was on guard
took a bite of my pear
flung it back in the yard,

as for the room, I went in
Andrew Borden was there
of course his smile was gone
n' when alive was quite rare...

I continued to the stairwell
to the guestroom where it led
I was halfway up the steps
when I looked at the bed,
on the floor by the dresser
where Mrs. Borden lay dead.

It was eerie, somewhat haunting
a scene of fright and dread
and sitting here today
the sight is branded in my head.

KNOWLTON: Now—
            if I may be so bold to ask
            when up the walk you came
            there were people all around
            you ignored them all the same
            went out back for a snack
            tell us…
            what was your game?

MORSE: I entered that dreadful place
            with a mood of lost despair
            of the man's broken face
            I was shocked and unaware,
            n' his poor battered wife
            a suspicious sad affair.

KNOWLTON: I am done with this witness
            this horseman nomad
            the defense can have at him
            his alibi's iron clad,
            he is yours, Mr. Jennings,
            I have nothing to add
            but pay heed to your proximity
            he smells like a horse real bad.

Cross-examination.

JENNINGS: I have only a few questions
            regarding the search and the meal
            allow me to get started
            before the blood can congeal,
            let's start with the spread
            and any truths you conceal
            was it true you love to eat
            and that breakfast was unreal?

MORSE: Of the breakfast I had
            it was apt for a king
            coffee, mutton n' bread
            of johnnycakes I must sing,
            bananas, broth, n' milk
            Mrs. Borden she did bring
            I did not scrimp or decline
            from that culinary fling.

JENNINGS: Now just for the record
             you know you've been sworn
             1860, would you say
             the year Lizzie was born,
             would that be correct
             or would that be wrong?

MORSE: As for the girl's right age
             it's not as simple you see
             not like counting the rings
             on the trunk of a tree,
             she could be 30
             or perhaps 33...
             now, if she be a horse
             in her mouth I could see
             by inspecting her teeth
             an age I could plea,
             n' tell you for certain
             the year she was born
             then we all could agree.

JENNINGS: Let's move forward—
             did you assist with the search
             escort the police around
             open chests, forage trunks
             was anything worth noting found?

MORSE: Police swarm n' hordes
             n' with total disregard
             the public did explore
             the barn, loft, and yard,
             a frenzy was n' display
             as children ran n' played
             on the fence and the drive
             despite the constabulary raid.

JENNINGS: Are you endeavoring to say
             it was all a parade?

MORSE: *(With a grimace.)*
             I think your interrogation
             my good man you misplace
             it's the police you need grill
             about the house they encase,
             I assisted with the search

as the killer made his escape
it's no bloody fault of mine
of the shroud of guilt n' hate,
and the fact we are all here
to witness Lizzie Borden's fate
is a waste of my good time
better things are on my plate
like the farm in where I live
or the horse I'd like to date.

JENNINGS: Very well...
I am finished with this witness
Your Honor I conclude
he's gotten quite upset
and is beginning to brood.

JUDGE: You may stand down, Mr. Morse
Prosecution, your next witness
with any evidence you have wooed.

JENNINGS returns to his station. HOSEA KNOWLTON, who is very businesslike and the most serious person in the room, stands and addresses the court.

KNOWLTON: I call one Bridget Sullivan.
BAILIFF: *(Summoning her in a boring tone.)* Forward, Miss Sullivan.

BRIDGET SULLIVAN, the Borden maid, starts for the stand, walking slowly and with great apprehension. She pauses and slowly looks back at LIZZIE, who gives her the same vacant stare she has for everyone. The lights in the room fade to black. One small light shines down on her.

BRIDGET: Oh...pshaw, pshaw,
should have never
unlatched that door
and let death be invited
on the sofa for the sitting
by the bed upon the floor.

From the lush grassy meadows
in the mist of a shamrock moon
lay the heaven I left behind
a harmony I must find
from this horror spun in time.

Oh, no more, no more
can I bear, or endure

the cut of the morning light
with hot kitchen embers
from a poisoned summer night,
must steal my heart's desire
to the rolling, knoll'ee field
where the Shannon River fills
where my heart will always heal,
by the hedgerows on the hills
and my sins God does forgive
of the secret I must not reveal.

Oh pshaw, pshaw,
death will endure here no more
when in this lock I place the key
that binds this sin to me,
unbolt a spirit I may steer
away from this devilish crypt
to escape all that I fear,
pshaw, pshaw
to unbar my own passion
to unlock my own door
pshaw, pshaw, pshaw.

The light returns and BRIDGET SULLIVAN takes the stand, looking frightened and uncertain, as she places her hand on the Bible held by the BAILIFF and is sworn in.

Direct-examination.

KNOWLTON: You're the housekeeper
the Borden's live-in maid
please don't be so timid
you should not be afraid,
now, please state your name
and where you reside,
oh yes, and I must ask
about an axe you may hide.

There's a pause. BRIDGET looks at KNOWLTON, then scans the room, stopping as her eyes lock with LIZZIE BORDEN's. She is frightened and anxious.

KNOWLTON: Relax my good woman
you have nothing to fear
all I really need to know

are you the assassin, my dear,
did you unlock the back door
and let the killer inside
did you hear a loud cry
did you take it in stride,
and can you bring to mind
if Lizzie laughed or she cried
was she cool as a cucumber
when her father had died?

BRIDGET: My name be Bridget Sullivan—
I'm a simple domestic
in this country to toil
from an old Ireland world
to clean up the soil
tinged by the rich
who you know are well spoiled.
I was summoned as Maggie
by Emma and Lizzie
where the Misses, Abby Borden,
would keep me quite busy,
where I would make up meals,
wash windows and such
but the bedrooms above
I was not to touch,
and as for an axe
and of blood on a dress
ignorance and stupidity
to the court I confess.

KNOWLTON: As Mrs. Borden instructed
you were washing the glass
and when the killer arrived
you had not seen him pass?

BRIDGET: I washed all the windows
as I circled the house,
saw no one come in
not even a mouse—
well...maybe a mouse.

KNOWLTON: What were your duties
the day of the crime
when Morse left the house
can you recall the time,

of Andrew Borden's return
or the clock you heard chime
from a nap you awoke
when Lizzie Borden did whine?

BRIDGET: Mrs. Borden gave instructions
the windows I should clean
and when I was finished
she was no longer seen,
then I heard Lizzie say
that she was given a note
for someone was sick
and into town she elope,
done with my burden
I went up to my bed
'till Lizzie did holler
come down, quick...
Father's dead.

KNOWLTON: Very well, Miss Sullivan,
before we resign
can you give us a schedule
can you set up the time,
the events of that day
to the best of your rhyme?

BRIDGET: We were all very sick
myself, I was ill
went to the backyard
near the bucket of swill,
to retch and to vomit
my insides I did spill.

KNOWLTON: So, that day you were ill?

BRIDGET: A headache did plague me
I was not feeling good
still, down into the cellar
I had gone for some wood,
to light the stove
make the meal as I should
despite my affliction
it was well understood.

KNOWLTON: And as a good servant
             you did as you should
             please continue, Miss S,
             this is sounding real good.

BRIDGET: Yes. It was half past six
             when Mrs. Borden came down
             Mr. Borden soon followed
             a slop pail and a frown,
             I made breakfast as always
             for Mr. Morse was aroun'
             and the smell of hot johnnycakes
             he could smell across town,
             I gathered the milk
             and prepared the cuisine
             and for coffee and cookies
             came Lizzie the Queen.

KNOWLTON: Now you claim you were ill
             and went up to your room
             and were not there for long
             let's say, sometime before noon,
             and when Lizzie did call
             you came down real soon.

             Now, did you see any blood
             on her hair or her dress
             did she look well composed
             or was the Queen in a mess,
             tell all that you know
             may revel or express?

BRIDGET: I was earning a nap
             till Miss Lizzie did call,
             "Maggie come down,"
             my name in the hall,
             "Father is dead
             on the couch he did fall."

             I ran down the stairs
             without even a snore
             I cannot rightly say
             the dress Lizzie wore
             was spotted with blood
             or anything more.

KNOWLTON: What was the dress
              Miss Lizzie Borden wore?

JENNINGS: Your Honor, we object
              to that question, we implore.

JUDGE: Overruled, Mr. Jennings,
              let it continue as before.

KNOWLTON: Was the dress pattern calico
              or was it more blue
              does it bring to your mind
              what I'm referring to?

BRIDGET: The dress was not calico
              but light blue with a sprig
              which was darker in color
              and on the caboose very big.

KNOWLTON: Did it contain light spots
              or any figures or dots?

JENNINGS: *(Jumping up from his seat in protest.)*
              This is very leading, now
              this inquiry must end
              stop milking this cow
              the bench must amend.

KNOWLTON: I have no more questions
              to the magistrate I defer
              the defense may rebut
              if that's what they prefer.

              Mr. Jennings may explore
              I've nothing else to add
              I give up the floor
              after giving all I have.

KNOWLTON returns to his station and sits, writes, then leans back in his chair chewing on his pencil. JENNINGS moves very slowly with poise and confidence. He pauses halfway as he approaches the witness, and in deep thought, stands a minute looking at the floor, an index finger up to his lips. As if coming out of a trance he begins his cross-examination.

Cross-examination.

JENNINGS: Good morning, Miss Sullivan,
                    lovely dress I am sure
                    you look very charming
                    makes a man want to purr.

BRIDGET: Nice for you to say so
                    I am grateful to you, Sir.

JENNINGS: Now, I need to ask—
                    in eating their meals
                    can you tell us in short
                    did they all eat together
                    will the evidence support,
                    the testimony you gave
                    from the inquest report?

BRIDGET: Can't remember the inquest
                    but, Emma ate at the table
                    they ate all together
                    or when Lizzie was able,
                    I could just have forgot
                    I can say or say not
                    not sure what to do
                    when placed on the spot.

JENNINGS: Let me stop you right there—
                    they did from time to time
                    then day to day, did they not
                    Lizzie and her parents
                    did not eat apart?

BRIDGET: They did... day to day
                    but time to time... I say not
                    they were not there you see
                    and at time there a lot,
                    and if you speak of the food
                    of the meat in the pot
                    of the fish and the mutton
                    well, they were served real hot.

JENNINGS: Did Lizzie not speak
                    that tempers were shot
                    that Andrew and Abby

a cold shoulder they got,
that her and Emma
staged mind games instead
that this all went on
till they all went to bed?

BRIDGET: Lizzie spoke kindly
to that I can say
with Abby she chat
though with little foreplay,
though they all never spoke
when she was away
and when I was not present
to that I can't say.

JENNINGS: Did you not mention earlier
that Lizzie did cry
when she discovered her father
or was that just a lie,
since it has been heard
that she shed no tears
what are we to believe
your deceit or our ears?

And upon Borden's return
you unlocked the front door
I understand it was jammed
you had no trouble before,
and you heard Lizzie laugh
at the top of the stair
after you gave Andrew entry
did you see her stand there?

BRIDGET: I know that I've mentioned
I said Lizzie did cry
I have been tutored and coached
be it truth or a lie,
till it all sounds to me
like pie in the sky.

This I can tell you
I unlocked the front door
Mr. Borden walked in
I can tell you no more,
I did not see her laughing

when I hollered, "pshaw"
of the coming and goings
I'm wise to ignore.

And allow me to plead
no killers had I seen
as I worked all about
from the barn n' between,
but the windows I washed
if it be one or thirteen
was a job well done
spotless and clean.

JENNINGS: I'm finished with this witness
can't say who is winning
since the witness has left us
with our brains dazed and spinning.

JUDGE: Very well, Mr. Jennings,
we will all take a break
(Slamming the gavel.)
we will adjourn till soon after
some coffee and cake.

*EVERYONE leaves the room. The only two people left are CLARENCE DARROW
and WILLIAM JENNINGS BRYAN. Lights lower and the room goes dark. The
focus is now on the two lawyers. BRYAN slams down his cards in irritation as
DARROW gathers and sweeps all the matchsticks in the pot his way.*

BLACKOUT

ACT II
Scene Two

The lights come up on the card table revealing CLARENCE DARROW and WILLIAM JENNINGS BRYAN continuing their discussion at the back of the room.

BYRAN: Bah!

DARROW: Relax! It's only the first hand, Bryan. It's not a final adjudication. Sullivan and Morse are down, but there are a lot more interesting witnesses.

BYRAN: You would think they could get something more substantial out of both Morse and the maid. She was there. I know she saw something, I know it. *(He studies his cards.)*

DARROW: Though both Sullivan and Morse showed promise, unfortunately it was fruitless for the prosecution.

BYRAN: I was hoping their testimony would be more damaging.

DARROW: I don't think it was damaging at all.

BYRAN: It served their purpose, I suppose.

DARROW: In what way?

BYRAN: The reason for calling Morse confirms his innocence, and in doing so, points the finger of guilt towards the real killer... Lizzie Borden. John Morse also witnessed Lizzie present and at the house the day of the crime.

DARROW: I don't know about that. Morse never saw Lizzie the morning of the crime.

BYRAN: He saw her the night before.

DARROW: It is my understanding that he may have heard her come in the night before, but never really witnessed her arrive.

BYRAN: Oh, believe me, Lizzie was there.

DARROW: You're steadfast, Bryan, if anything. I'll give you that.

BYRAN: Just following the facts.

DARROW: What was the prosecution's benefit for calling Bridget Sullivan, if the maid really never had anything of benefit to offer?

BYRAN: She was of some benefit—proving that Lizzie lied about Abby receiving a note—about dissension between the daughters and their parents.

DARROW: Correction, counselor. Bridget Sullivan never gave a clear reply to the question of whether the family ate together—and about the note, just indicated she never saw one, that was all.

BYRAN: That will have to be enough. After all, there was no note.

DARROW: Well, that is what the prosecution wishes us to believe. That Lizzie is lying about the note... thus ditto, as to the murder itself.

BYRAN: She also testified that when she went upstairs for a nap she saw Andrew Borden and Lizzie alive. Minutes later one of them was dead. *(He drops his cards on the table, face up.)* All diamonds!

DARROW: *(Fanning his cards, he places them down.)* Not good enough!

BYRAN: Damn. I had a good hand. I was certain I had you.

DARROW: Well, it will be a long trial.

BYRAN: You were darting your eyes, tapping your fingers. You appeared quite nervous.

DARROW: It's what is known as a bluff, part of the gambit which adds such color and enthusiasm to this entertaining but wicked pastime, as you would call it.

BYRAN: How the hell did you beat that? *(Pointing at his cards with an open hand.)*

DARROW: *(Counting his matchsticks.)* You can't flush out a full house, my friend.

BYRAN: I should have seen it coming. I must admit, the Morse and Sullivan testimonies were nothing more than ambiguous.

DARROW: A providential horse trader and an archetypal servant girl? You know, the prosecuting attorney reminded me of a young William Jennings Bryan I once knew.

BYRAN: I take that as a compliment.

DARROW: As you should.

BYRAN: Let's look at this more closely.

DARROW: The hand I played?

BYRAN: The case. The case. Why do you think we are here?

DARROW: Such a case speaks to us. That is why we are here. We have been handed the case of an elderly man and his wife, both murdered in the light of day, on a busy street, in their own home, and the youngest daughter prejudicially charged with the heinous crime.

BYRAN: Ambushed, presumably, with the same weapon, an hour or more apart.

DARROW: Right! It was a very sultry day in August, the fourth to be exact, and as I understand, the only souls in that house to survive the massacre were Liz, and the maid, Bridget.

BYRAN: We must not forget John Morse.

DARROW: Well, as he made clear through his testimony, he was not at the house at the time.

BYRAN: Yes, but he slept in the very bedroom where Abby Borden's body was discovered. For God's sake, the man was considered a suspect at one time. You would think he would have given up vital testimony. I am certain he was holding back.

DARROW: *(Stacking his matchsticks in a neat pile.)* That may be so. But as you heard, he had a water-tight alibi.

BYRAN: Rubbish!

DARROW: I know, his testimony was nothing short of a defense of himself.

BYRAN: The man was a poor witness, I concede that.

DARROW: It was my understanding that the oldest daughter, Emma, was away in Fairhaven, just a couple of miles from the house. What do you have to say about that?

BYRAN: How convenient.

DARROW: She was not in Fall River. That is all that counts.

BYRAN: Come now, she knew something was brewing. She just wanted to be out of the way. If you ask me, her trip to Fairhaven was a practice in machination, true and simple.

DARROW: You're too cynical. Now let's get back to the events of that day. Andrew Borden left the house, when?

BYRAN: Around nine in the morning—he and Morse.

DARROW: That left the stepmother, maid, and Liz at home.

BYRAN: Supposedly... though Lizzie claims that her stepmother received a note— that she had gone out. That's what she testified to at the inquest—and told her father. She stands by the story even today.

DARROW: Interesting. So you are implying that Liz lied—that the stepmother never went out and no note was ever delivered.

BYRAN: I believe Lizzie Borden fabricated the story since Abby Borden was already dead—made it up so no one would go searching for the dead woman.

DARROW: That's assuming that Liz perpetrated the crime?

BYRAN: What's with this pet name you have given her? Her name is Lizzie not Liz.

DARROW: I like... Liz. She reminds me of a Liz I used to know. Same spunk. You know when I was a child I had a pet snake named Liz.

BYRAN: That's the problem with you, Clarence, you empathize with clients whether they are guilty or not, you make them your pets.

DARROW: We are attorneys. We get paid to find the guilty innocent and the innocent guilty.

BYRAN: Always changing the subject. Can we get on with this?

DARROW: *(Clears his throat.)* So someone kills the old lady, which leaves Liz and the maid alone in the house.

BYRAN: Well, yes and no.

DARROW: Meaning?

BYRAN: Both women have reported leaving the house to go into the yard. The maid to wash the windows, and, if we are to believe Lizzie, her visit to the barn. Either way, if someone were to go into the house they would need to get by both women without being seen.

DARROW: Was the back screen door not locked?

BYRAN: Aagh! A simple door fastener, not much bigger than a fishing hook. *(He picks up DARROW's straw hat and fans himself.)*

DARROW: I see what you mean. A hooked screen door is not much deterrent to a killer. But the door was undamaged. Perhaps the intruder entered when Liz was in the barn.

BYRAN: Nonsense. She was never in the barn.

DARROW: Then how did the killer get in?

BYRAN: He didn't need to.

DARROW: How is that possible?

BYRAN: Because the assassin came from inside that house.

DARROW: I don't believe that.

BYRAN: A perpetrator would have no place to hide once he was in the house. It was a tiny cramped building.

DARROW: How do you know.? Have you been inside?

BYRAN: I don't need to.

DARROW: You have been reading too much fiction, my good man. The house was not small—in fact, it was large—three whole levels. There were many places a killer could have hidden—bedroom closets, hallway closet, under the front stairs, the basement. Under the maid's bed—in the maid's bed.

BYRAN: Get serious, Clarence. Highly unlikely, if not improbable—the murders were committed over an hour apart. Abby at 9:30 and her husband just before 11:00. What are we to think? That the trespasser killed the wife then hid for an hour waiting for the husband?

DARROW: Yes, why not?

BYRAN: Aagh! Doesn't make sense. How did the killer know what time Andrew Borden would be back, or if he was even in town? No, no... the killer was quite aware of the goings and comings—because she lived in that house.

DARROW: She?

BYRAN: To echo Lizzie's guilt—let me add that we know she was upstairs in her bedroom at least part of the time that morning. She would have to walk up and down the front stairway and should have seen Abby Borden in the guest bedroom.

DARROW: Perhaps she didn't look that way. She could have been looking down... at her feet.

BYRAN: Ha!

DARROW: Why not? I look down at my feet when I'm taking the stairs.

BYRAN: If you're in your own home you know every step. No need to look.

DARROW occupies his time building a house of cards.

DARROW: All right! If she did kill the stepmother she would have plenty of time to get rid of the weapon and wash off the blood. I give you that. But if she killed her father, it is impossible for the maid to have seen Andrew Borden alive then dead ten to fifteen minutes later, and for Liz to be the murderer and have no blood on her. There was just not enough time for her to wash it off... and believe me, there was plenty of blood—none of it on her clothes, her face, her hair. And what of the axe? How did she get rid of it? Where did it go?

BYRAN: She didn't. They have it here as exhibit number one.

DARROW: You have seen it?

BYRAN: I have.

DARROW: It's just a simple carpenter's hatchet with a broken, and if I may emphasize, missing handle. You don't really believe that to be the implement?

BYRAN: She broke the handle on Borden's skull and threw it into the kitchen stove where she burnt it.

DARROW: Come now, are you serious? Have you ever broken a handle off an axe or a hatchet, or tried to?

BYRAN: Why... yes, as a young man—not intentionally.

DARROW: Then you know it is not an easy task and highly unlikely, for a woman to break a hatchet handle on a brittle facial skeleton of an old man. How in the world can you conclude she is guilty of that?

BYRAN: She had motive. Who else could have done it?

Appearing disinterested, DARROW begins to fling playing cards across the courtroom.

DARROW: Perhaps the old man and his wife killed each other.

BYRAN: *(Slamming the straw hat on the table.)* Damn you, Clarence. There are two people dead and you jest.

DARROW: Calm, Bryan, calm. You have always had the propensity to lose composure. It will cost you a case or two, if not an election one day.

BYRAN: Sorry! Since coming off that Scopes trial a couple of days ago it is taking me some time to decompress.

DARROW: I understand. But outbursts of emotion have no ranking in the occupation of a bully attorney such as yourself.

BYRAN: All right, all right, let's get on with it.

DARROW: Now, we agree that Bridget Sullivan was washing windows at the time of Abby's death. We can concur that she was in the house when Borden was murdered.

BYRAN: Who knows. She could be lying. Perhaps she is in on it. At this point anything is possible.

DARROW: Was she not in the barn when the old man was killed?

BYRAN: No, no! That was Lizzie. Lizzie's alibi. She claimed that she went into the barn. The maid was in her bedroom, napping.

DARROW: Oh yes, I remember now. So Liz went to the barn. To do what, again?

BYRAN: For some lead for fishing sinkers, or some tin or iron to repair a screen or something. Have you not been listening? I thought you knew this case.

DARROW: Wait! Did you say fishing?

BYRAN: I did.

DARROW: Well, if she likes fishing she can't be all bad, can she now?

DARROW leans back in his chair and folds his hands behind his neck, rocking. The chair's front legs hover off the floor.

DARROW: What a treasure—a woman angler.

BYRAN: Please, Clarence, focus man. This is no trivial matter.

CLARENCE DARROW jumps out of the chair and to his feet. His disposition becomes serious and his voice booming. A cool composure suddenly becomes animated.

DARROW: I am focused, my dear Bryan. And no, it is not trivial, as you put it. Death is never trivial. Life, on the other hand, of little or no consequence.

BYRAN: *(Crossing his arms and nodding.)* Oh no! Here we go...again.

DARROW: One may be starved, plagued with a great social and racial injustice, or have one's body violated by a madman or a debilitating disease. These things are of minor deliberation. But death, death on the other hand... of considerable prominence, never trivial. Thus is practiced the perversion of man's treatment of man. Mankind's misplaced priority, to live with the injustice of the living, but never the inequity of the dead. Thereby death is paramount, since it carries judicial salvation and fairness from the grave to the bench, while the living are left to defend truth and equity of character on their own merits. What significant and preordained value the dead have over the living.

BYRAN stares at him in a moment of silence.

BYRAN: Do you yield, counselor, or are you going to carry on?

DARROW: Just trying to set the record straight. *(Sits back down.)*

BYRAN: Can we continue?

DARROW: Where were we?

BYRAN: While her father was being killed, Lizzie Borden said she was in the barn loft looking for some sinkers. She is not really clear, since her alibi has changed several times.

DARROW: I thought she was in the yard eating pears?

BYRAN: Yes, that too.

DARROW: *(Somewhat detached, he examines his cuticle and nails and bites at them.)* Go on?

BYRAN: Whatever story you choose to believe, it is all embellishment, a cover up, a lie on Lizzie's part.

DARROW: And Bridget Sullivan?

BYRAN: As for the servant girl, she claims to have been in her bedroom, on the third floor, at the rear of the house, napping, while Andrew Borden was being liquidated.

DARROW: Liquidated... I like that—very descriptive, Bryan. You should use that term in deliberations.

Not happy with the sarcasm, BYRAN gives DARROW a look of displeasure.

BYRAN: Not long after Andrew Borden is killed, the blood still pumping, Lizzie yells up for the maid to come down, that "someone has killed Father," or something to that effect.

DARROW: Bridget Sullivan heard nothing beforehand?

BYRAN: Nothing.

DARROW: Something is not right there.

BYRAN: You can say that.

DARROW: I find it difficult to swallow that Bridget Sullivan's memory could be that scant. She was much too vague on the stand, almost like she was holding something back.

BYRAN: Holding a lot back.

DARROW: To be honest, I must conclude her testimony was problematic. Especially for the prosecution.

BYRAN: To say the least.

DARROW: One moment she said Liz did not always eat with her parents, then shortly after she suffers a complete mental lapse, claiming she did.

BYRAN: The same is true of the inquest story, of whether she witnessed Lizzie shedding tears when her father was discovered dead. Very contrary to what she testified to on the stand.

DARROW: You know, I can sympathize with the young lady.

BYRAN: Yea, you would.

DARROW: No. Let's look at this from her perspective. She's a simple-minded, Irish, farm girl in a strange country, in the middle of a murder case, and she is being lobbied by attorneys left and right, all who have little interest in her welfare, all trying to instill in her the words she should say in court. The poor girl is torn.

BYRAN: So?

DARROW: So, her story on the stand becomes confusing, so what?

BYRAN: Don't trust her. She's protecting someone.

DARROW: I don't trust her entirely myself. Yet, it's an advantage to the defense that she admits as little as possible. I would have to concede that she told the truth, best she could.

BYRAN: That's because you really believe Lizzie Borden is guilty.

DARROW: I never said that. *(Leans over and gives BRYAN a smirk.)*

BYRAN: I cannot see how Bridget Sullivan will be of much value to the prosecution. Both her and Morse... two pears in the same basket.

DARROW: Cheer up, my good man, there are more pears and other baskets to rummage through.

BYRAN: *(Looking glum.)* That's the calamity and uncertainty behind this Godless and evil crime.

DARROW: For you perhaps... one litigant's calamity is another's parade.

BYRAN: Doesn't make it right.

DARROW: Come now, Bryan, neither one of us ride snowy horses or wear white hats. We may litigate with clean hands, but few of us allow those limbs to become soiled with the sweat and blood of the client, be they guilty or not. You and I, Sir, are no saints. After all, did literature not see our profession with a dim eye? Did it not proclaim that all the lawyers should be killed?

BYRAN: Sentiments of a rogue Elizabethan, not an American. It is a beacon which you shine on yourself. Don't include me in it.

DARROW: You sound bitter. *(Trying to balance his straw hat off his nose.)* But take comfort my friend, for if God be on your side, I am certain He has already informed you of the outcome.

BYRAN: I know the outcome, damn it. *(Jumps from his chair and begins to pace the floor.)* That's what I'm here for. To change it. You have no conscience at times, Clarence, heedlessly defending killers, rapists, and fornicators of law—using your dull agnostic humor to injure and insult. *(Shouting.)* What of the innocent? What of their rights? Tell me, Sir, what of the innocent.

DARROW: If we are all defenders of the innocent, who would speak for the presumed guilty? Was not your God nailed to a tree for the sins and infractions of the truly guilty?

BYRAN: Your point?

DARROW: That I am a more pious man than you give credit.

BYRAN: Perhaps we should just forget this scheme of ours—this card game... it's morally insensitive to say the least.

DARROW: Morality, ethics, life, death, win, lose, how can we count it all in the end, eh? William Jennings Bryan, defender of God and Justice, and Clarence Darrow, champion of assassins and debauchery. In the eyes of God, you are Able and I Cain. Let the chips fall where they may, Bryan. After all, if you quit now nothing in this case will change. Put it in the hands of God, as you would implore.

BYRAN: My agreement to this little game of cards was in error, both on judicial and religious grounds. *(Throws himself back into the chair in defeat. He begins to reflect.)* Did you know that the Romans played cards to see who would get the possessions of Christ while he hung on the cross, Clarence?

DARROW: I think they rolled dice. But that's neither here nor there.

BYRAN: Cards, dice, it's all the same. Games of the devil.

DARROW: You have no confidence in your ability... your skill in turning it all around, do you? If you play with that temperament it will be the trial that decides who wins our little game of cards, instead of the other way around.

BYRAN: Aagh!

DARROW: If you wish, we will quit, in which case Lizzie Borden wins and God loses.

DARROW takes a fresh deck of cards from his pocket and flings them on the table. After a short pause, BRYAN picks them up and tears at the wrapper.

BYRAN: All right, let's get to it.

DARROW: Three out of five.

BYRAN: Until one of us is broke.

DARROW: Now you're talking.

BYRAN: Why in hell did I come here? *(Shuffles cards.)* I could have been enjoying the cool breezes in the south of France. Instead, I find myself in this hot, impoverished, Godforsaken, rundown, fishing town.

DARROW: *(Rubbing his hands together.)* If the preponderance of the game goes your way, then Lizzie Borden hangs. If I prevail, she walks free.

BYRAN: I know, I know. After this game is done and over, you don't really believe that she will be found innocent, do you?

DARROW: I never said innocent. *(Broad smile.)* I said free. History has already decided on a conclusive resolution. The question is, can we discover any new evidence here today that may have been overlooked in 1893, and will our actions change the outcome?

BYRAN: *(Dealing cards.)* She did it. Lizzie Borden killed her stepmother and elderly father.

DARROW: I think you're grasping for straws.

BYRAN: Lizzie Borden is guilty and I must try my best to make history see the injustice that has been handed down through time.

DARROW: May the best man win.

CLARENCE DARROW lights a cigarette and chuckles. His laughter echoes throughout the courtroom mingling with the sound of a banging gavel. The lights brighten. The case resumes.

BLACKOUT

ACT II
Scene Three

The case continues under brightened lights, as the JUDGE gives instruction and KNOWLTON prepares the direct examination of ADELAIDE CHURCHILL.

JUDGE: Can we hear the next witness,
                      Mr. Knowlton, proceed,
                      Bailiff, get out the Bible
                      and read them the creed.

KNOWLTON: Miss Adelaide Churchill,
                      I hail to the floor,
                      the first to see Lizzie
                      where she lived next door,
                      now, what she will tell us
                      may cut to the core
                      and from her gossipy lips
                      Lizzie's guilt I will draw.

ADELAIDE BUFFINGTON CHURCHILL is sworn in.

Direct-examination.

KNOWLTON: Your name, my dear woman,
                      can you inform the court
                      we know your papa was mayor
                      but please keep it short.

CHURCHILL: My name is Adelaide Churchill
                      but you may all call me Addie
                      you'll find me genial and friendly
                      not cheeky or crabby.

KNOWLTON: Now, Addie, address the jury
                      about that terrible day
                      the events of the hour
                      and of Lizzie's ballet?

CHURCHILL: I did not notice much dancing
                      when by the window I stood
                      where I spied a sad Lizzie
                      things were not as they should.

I asked, "Lizzie, what's the matter,"
she cried, "Mrs. Churchill, do come,"
Some one has killed father,
he looks senseless and numb."

So I ran right on over
to lend some support
her hand I did hold
despite blister or wart.

I asked where is your father,
"in the sitting room," she said
and you when it happened,
"in the barn for some lead."

And where is your mother
"she got a note," she replied
that "someone was sick"
or "someone had died."

She continued to add,
"Father has enemies, you know,
I heard Abby come in
or the sound of a blow."

KNOWLTON: That's all very humble
that you were very kind
but interesting it is not
so what else did you find?

CHURCHILL: I scurried down Second Street
to Mr. Hall's stable
and begged for a man
to get a doctor, if able,

then I stopped by the window
of Elsie Ann's chic boutique
where they were holding a sale
on a gown I found unique.

It had ruffles and pearls
made of silk and Indian lace
like those worn at an opera
by that singer, I forget her face,

but it had those fashionable sleeves
leg of mutton I think they're called, then I...

KNOWLTON: *(Interrupts, shouting.)*
              Stop, stop, Mrs. Churchill,
              and focus on the lines
              the ones in which I'm asking
              and not your clothes designs.

CHURCHILL: Sorry, I just thought
              you'd like to know,
              but if...

KNOWLTON: To that I would say, *(Shouts.)* No!

CHURCHILL: Well, I never...

KNOWLTON: Now—
              you visited Hall's Stable
              for a doctor to ensnare
              was there a doctor soon to follow
              at the house when you got there?

CHURCHILL: No, but—
              when I returned to the place
              found Doc Bowen eating a pear
              Bridget the maid was present
              oh, what a ghastly affair
              and if it were a church
              I would kneel down to prayer.

KNOWLTON: Let me stop you right there
              and move onto the dress
              the one Lizzie wore
              during the butchery fest.

              (Holding a dark blue dress in his hand.)

              Now, my dear lady,
              was this the attire
              which Lizzie did wear
              of you I inquire,
              on the day of the crime
              when she did conspire
              to kill her parents
              with rage and desire?

CHURCHILL: Can't say it is
for I'd be a liar.

KNOWLTON: *(Waving her away in displeasure.)*
No more questions, Your Honor,
of this witness I tire.

ANDREW JENNINGS springs to his feet.

Cross-examination.

JENNINGS: You're a busy woman, I gather
but can you tell us if you please
the dress Lizzie had worn
was it a two piece or chemise,
was it the color of the ocean
or the hue on the trees
and the one the maid don
was it made to stir or to tease?

CHURCHILL: I can state quite clearly
the dress Lizzie wore
was a calico blue
or like one inside the store,
the one worn by the maid
I can't profess, I adore
since I cannot recollect
took notes or kept the score.

JENNINGS: Alice Russell was there
a friend—is that right,
can you describe her garb
was it dreary or bright?

CHURCHILL: The only outfit I recall
was the one I had on
it was a colorful number
of silk and chiffon
you know, I purchased that dress
on a vacation in St. John
with Mildred and Hattie
of whom I'm quite fond,
it was a splendid spring day
we took a ride by the pond
and afterwards we...

JENNINGS interrupts her.

JENNINGS: Let's move on, Mrs. Churchill,
                      talk of stains on the dress
                      which the axe did splatter
                      when the blade did molest,
                      did you see any blood
                      that the garment possess
                      on her hands or her face
                      was her conduct a mess?

CHURCHILL: I did not see blood,
                      splatter, or stain
                      on her collar or waist
                      to the hem, all was plain.

JENNINGS: Let's talk of the note
                      can you recount or refill
                      the one Abby was given
                      stating someone was ill?

CHURCHILL: I was told by Bridget
                      of this she did tell
                      Abby was given a note
                      that a friend was unwell.

JENNINGS: Exactly what did she say
                      when she told you the tale
                      did you hear it from Lizzie
                      what this note did entail?

CHURCHILL: I did not hear it from Lizzie
                      but from the maid instead
                      that Abby was dusting
                      and making the bed,
                      when the note had arrived
                      that she would lose her head
                      but we couldn't be quite sure
                      until it was all done and said.

JENNINGS: *(Looking at JUROR.)*
                      Dreadful oration
                      this plot we churn

> *(Turning to JUDGE.)*
> I have no more inquiry
> I concede and adjourn.
>
> *(Turns to CHURCHILL.)*
> Mrs. Churchill, you may go shopping
> for a gown we all can burn.

JUDGE: Call the next witness.
Mr. Knowlton, your turn.

ALICE RUSSELL comes forward. She looks coolheaded and confident. The BAILIFF holds out the Bible as she walks by. She taps it with conviction, ignores him, and continues walking, parroting the words "I do." The BAILIFF shakes his head in tedious boredom and prances away. ALICE RUSSELL, the prosecution's star witness, takes the stand and immediately begins her testimony—without waiting for questions.

Direct-examination.

RUSSELL: Now, Mr. Knowlton,
please state your age
of this crime you do try
what's your fee, what's your wage?

KNOWLTON: Now, now, Miss Russell,
it does not work that way
I ask all the questions
for which you must obey.

RUSSELL: Sorry, Mr. Knowlton,
never done this before.

KNOWLTON: I forgive you, dear lady,
just don't do it anymore.

RUSSELL: I'm ready now, dear man,
any questions you may draw
you may proceed at leisure
flap your lips, move your jaw.

KNOWLTON: Please, Miss Russell,
give me a chance to speak
and don't interrupt
when the questions I tweak.

RUSSELL: It will not happen again
you see, I live alone
often talk to myself
since I don't have a phone,
if I could just find a man
that I could call my own
a lover or a butcher
to throw me a bone
before I get too old
and they call me a crone.

KNOWLTON: I understand, Miss Russell,
but let me set the tone.

Now, I'm afraid to ask
yet I need to try
tell us where you live
any facts that apply.

RUSSELL: I have lived in Fall River
for many a year
I'm a friend of Miss Lizzie
but not for long, I fear.

KNOWLTON: You met with the accused
the night before the crime
can you tell us what was said
can you advise of the place and time?

RUSSELL: Lizzie came to me at home
and stayed until nine
and if she were a man
it would have been so divine
for a man, a man
some day I must find.

KNOWLTON: Continue, Miss Russell,
just the facts of the crime.
stop driving us mad
I'm losing my mind.

RUSSELL: My apology, you win
let me see, where to begin?

When I spoke to Lizzie

she was sick with dread
afraid she was poisoned
by the milk and the bread,

For she had heard it said
Father had an enemy in town
she was afraid when in bed
they would burn the house down.

KNOWLTON: Now, there was talk of robbery
into the house they did roam
stealing items of value
when no one was at home.

RUSSELL: A break-in was discovered
stealing a watch and some money
and nothing was recovered
don't you think that sounds funny?

KNOWLTON: Can you tell us some more
since you and Lizzie were chummy?

RUSSELL: She said, "Father is rude
Doc Bowen he abused
it was shameful and crude
I was appalled and bemused,"
that's what she said
her integrity was bruised.

KNOWLTON: And on the day
of hatchet and blade
of blood and carnage
and the call by the maid
tell us if you please
of Lizzie Borden's charade.

RUSSELL: On August the fourth,
Bridget Sullivan dropped by
that someone was hurt
that someone may die.

Well, when I got to the house
Lizzie was sitting in a chair
Mrs. Churchill was fanning
her chin, nose, and hair.

KNOWLTON:	And did you talk to the girl
	were any inquiries made
	was she calm and serene
	did her nerves appear frayed?

RUSSELL:	I asked, "Lizzie can you tell me
	when your father was slain
	where did you flee?"
	"to the barn" she'd exclaimed,
	"I was looking around
	for some iron or tin
	till father was found
	his face all pushed in.

KNOWLTON:	Now, Miss Russell,
	let's get to the cream
	the reason you're here
	and what you have seen,
	of garments on fire
	evidence that was burned
	of blood on a dress
	and what you have learned.

RUSSELL:	The following Sunday
	Lizzie tore up a dress,
	"what are you doing" was the cry
	Emma asked she confess.
	Lizzie's impish reply
	to her sister's complaint
	"I'm going to burn this old thing
	it is covered with paint."

KNOWLTON:	Very well, Miss Russell,
	of this dress and it's tint
	can you tell us the style
	can you give us a hint?

RUSSELL:	It was a cheap simple dress
	a Bedford cord, I believe
	a light blue, I would add
	was the color of the weave.

| KNOWLTON: | Hmm, this is all very interesting |

this finger of fault and blame
of the dress Lizzie burned
of the blood, in the flame.

Pause. KNOWLTON walks back to his station.

She's all yours, Mr. Jennings,
this incriminating dame
and if I say so myself
Miss Lizzie she defame,
and if she should prattle on
of her search for a man
assist the poor woman
lend what aid that you can.

Cross-examination.

JENNINGS: Good morning, Miss Russell...
now, of that blue dress
did you see any blood
that you may assess,
was there a splatter or sprinkle
of brain matter or snot
a blood splotch that showered
before the plasma could clot?

I suppose what I'm asking
was there a dash or a speck
of blood on her person
a blotch, stain, or fleck.

RUSSELL: Of blood not a trace
in her hair or her clothes
on her face or her hands
she was clean as a rose,
I'm thorough you see
you can tell by my nose
and of that I am certain

(looking over at Knowlton)
it's just the way it goes.

(Speaking quickly.)
So if you have a cousin
a brother, foe or friend
an eligible bachelor

that you highly recommend,
in need of some loving
or a heart on the mend
you may send him my way
and my affections I will lend.

JENNINGS: That's all, Miss Russell,
you may now descend
and good luck in the hunt
for a man to befriend.

The JUDGE's gavel slams against its sounding block.

BLACKOUT

ACT II
Scene Four

The JUDGE's gavel slams against its sounding block. The only light present is a small beam illuminating DARROW and BRYAN in the back of the courtroom. DARROW cautiously glances up through his bushy eyebrows to the portrait of Abraham Lincoln hanging on the wall above BRYAN's head. In the picture glass he can plainly see that BRYAN is holding four sevens and the ace of hearts. DARROW, whose cards sit face down on the table, lifts the corner of each one and grimaces. He is one card short of a straight flush.

DARROW: *(Low tone of voice.)* Well, well! It looks like Mr. Lincoln is holding some serious armament.

BRYAN: *(A twitching smile flickers on his face.)* What was that you say?

DARROW: Aha... Alice Russell. I must concede she... *(Pauses, his hand resting on his cards.)*

BRYAN: Yes! Go on.

Though DARROW knows he has lost this hand, he tortures BRYAN, slowly turning over one card at a time, and tossing them onto the table. He drops the last card to BRYAN's delight. A dilated smile swells on BRYAN's face.

DARROW: A hand of dead soldiers.

BRYAN: Finally, the tide recedes.

DARROW: Bravo, Bryan. I told you your luck would turn.

BRYAN: *(Sweeping the matchsticks in the pot his way.)* I can thank Alice Russell for that. Lizzie Borden prepare for retribution.

DARROW: *(Looking over his losing hand.)* "Ten soldiers wisely led beat a hundred without a head."

BRYAN: Meaning?

DARROW: *(Wiping his face with his handkerchief.)* Oh, just a little quote by my little Greek friend. It was a good hand Miss Russell played... very brave.

BYRAN: A first class defense is not a matter of having a good hand, Clarence, but of playing a poor hand well.

DARROW: Alice Russell... damning testimony for sure.

BRYAN: It was her declaration which convinced the grand jury to bring this case to trial in the first place.

DARROW: Nonetheless, though it was damaging in principle it is circumstantial in practice.

BRYAN: Are we being a sore loser, Clarence?

DARROW: Not so. All we know is what she testified to. She saw no blood on the dress Liz destroyed, and we no longer have the dress as evidence. The police searched that house from pebble to splinter and a bloody dress was never discovered. Alice Russell's testimony is conjectural to say the least.

BRYAN: Clarence, I won that hand and there is no taking it away from me.

DARROW: A battle won does not a war procure. Knowlton will need a lot more than a burning dress they can't produce nor prove having blood on it.

BRYAN: Don't you worry, it's coming.

DARROW: From who, Seabury Bowen?

BRYAN: Can you think of any witnesses of higher repute than a physician?

DARROW: We will see. Bring on the doctors and deal the cards.

As BRYAN deals the JUDGE's gavel can be heard in the far distance. Bang, bang, bang. It gets louder and louder as the light in the courtroom gets brighter. Soon the room is illuminated, EVERYONE is at their stations, DOCTOR SEABURY BOWEN has been sworn in, and his testimony has begun.

Direct-examination.

BOWEN: My name is Seabury Bowen
and I live across the street
from the Borden's and their daughters
on that day of great heat.

When I arrived at the house
it was a scene of despair
Lizzie was seated comfortably
with a serene haunting stare.

It was then that I inquired
and Miss Lizzie sadly tell,
"Father was stabbed by a killer
with an axe he brought from hell."

I then went to the sitting room
the bloody site did repulse
to satisfy my curiosity
I felt for a pulse,
making certain the man expired
I examined inside his head
there was no eye, cheek or nose
but a large hole there instead.

KNOWLTON: Let's speak of the dress—
              in reference to color
              can you recite or assess
              the change in her attire,
              to you I must press
              did she go to her chamber
              another dress to possess?

BOWEN: Lizzie did change her garment
              after going up to her room
              a pink wrapper she wore
              a morning dress, I assume.

KNOWLTON: Let me interrupt you, Sir,
              Doctor, must we allow
              that during the inquest
              you were fibbing somehow,
              of the first dress you saw
              at the time you did vow
              in describing the color
              could it have been calico?

BOWEN: I'm not a man of fashion
              but I can say it was drab
              the color was indefinite
              a common stitch, I should add.

KNOWLTON: *(Exhibiting the blue dress.)*
              Is this what you call drab
              this dress in my hand
              and is this the blue dress
              can you tell me my good man?

JENNINGS: Wait a minute doctor. Judge, we object.

JUDGE: Overruled, Mr. Jennings, the objection you direct.

KNOWLTON: Again, my good Doctor,
              does it look like the dress
              that you have described
              at the earlier inquest?

BOWEN: It was ordinarily unattractive
              not much color or fluoresce
              more than that I can't say,
              volunteer, or express.

KNOWLTON: Answer the question
              was the dress drab or bright
              dark blue or calico
              I demand more insight?

BOWEN: I don't pretend to note color
              it was common, that I vow
              and to describe a girl's dress
              I cannot then or can I now.

KNOWLTON: Would you say it was drab
              now, Doctor, was it blue
              a morning calico dress
              would you say that it's true,
              of this dress in my hand
              can you give us a clue?

JENNINGS: We beg of the court
              once again, I must lead
              this is the government's own witness
              his inquiry does exceed,
              I can give reasonable latitude
              but this is more than we need
              and to this scrutiny we object
              this witness he does bleed.

KNOWLTON: I waive the question
              and I'll readdress,
              tell us, Doc Bowen,
              what color is this dress?

BOWEN: I've disclosed all I knew
              but if you really want to know
              I should call it dark blue.

KNOWLTON: *(Upset.)* Mr. Jennings, if you please
              from this witness you may draw
              you can now cross-examine
              I relinquish the floor.

ANDREW JENNINGS approaches BOWEN.

Cross-examination.

JENNINGS: Good morning, Doctor—
              can you please brief the court

---

about the telegram you sent
who you saw and so forth
following the egregious event?

BOWEN: When I arrived at the house
an observation I had made
of Miss Russell and Mrs. Churchill
of my wife and the maid
they were fanning Miss Lizzie
in the chair where she laid.

JENNINGS: Continue if you will, dear doctor,
of where you've gone or went
of any phone calls you have made
or telegraphs you sent.

BOWEN: Lizzie Borden, she did beg
for me to send a telegraph
a message I went out to send
on her request and her behalf.

JENNINGS: I bet your horse is very fast
though he's not a thoroughbred
to the office for a telegraph
in your buggy you quickly fled.

BOWEN: You may contend my horse is fast
when he starts his stride and pace
and as for the doctors yearly sprint
I've never lost a race.

I sent a telegraph as you say
to Emma Borden in Fairhaven
Informed her of the tragic news
a communique' that she was cravin'.

JENNINGS: Now, doctor, when you did return
from your trip with the sun and heat
did anyone else see Mr. Borden
or was he covered with a sheet?

BOWEN: I had asked Addie to come and see
Mr. Borden lying there
I lifted the sheet for her to look
but she declined and didn't care,

so upstairs I went to see dear Abby
where she laid in the bedroom lair
since two unhappy campers
said that she was lying there.

JENNINGS: Did Doctor Dolan assist you
in the guest bedroom above
to inspect the body which was dead
perform the duties that you love?

BOWEN: I arrived, and entered from the hall
she lay by the bureau and the bed
you could see that someone took an axe
and chop, chop, chopped her head.

JENNINGS: And as for Lizzie—
what service did you provide
what attention had you paid?

BOWEN: Bromo of caffeine was given to Lizzie
I administered it as first aid
to the dead man's feeble daughter
which she required, I'm afraid.

JENNINGS: Allow me to inquire
did you administer morphine
when Miss Lizzie was excited
was not that the routine?

BOWEN: She received a shot on Friday
for her nerves which were frail
continued up until the hearing
an ample dose without fail.

JENNINGS: Now, my good doctor—
does morphine effect the mind
can it twist all your thoughts
hallucinate and malign
where truth and perception
leave events lost in time?

BOWEN: When you speak to Miss Lizzie
her reply you may doubt
whether at the government inquest
or in a courtroom with clout.

JENNINGS: Are you trying to tell us
               she is not heartless or rude
               and it was the morphine, the drug
               which calibrated her mood?

BOWEN: The morphine she was given
               may spawn her to spout
               an insensitive ill nature
               and provoke her to pout
               but it was the morphine talking
               and not this sensitive girl scout.

               Of the drug she was given
               she may or not tell a lie
               ask a question if you wish
               but the lady's soaring high
               she may tell you the truth
               or stumble on an alibi
               and if she appeared quite aloof
               well, now you sure know why.

JENNINGS: I have no more questions.

JUDGE: Your next witness, Mr. Knowlton

KNOWLTON: Police, police, I need a fuzz
               is there ever one on hand
               when a murder is applied
               they're on a picnic in Japan...

               I beg the court's permission now
               to call an officer off his beat
               to be here with us today
               I summon one Marshal Fleet.

*ASSISTANT MARSHAL JOHN FLEET makes his appearance. He walks with
confidence and authority, his hat in his hand, pumping and bouncing on one
foot then the other—up and down, up and down, as if one leg was much longer
then its sibling. While he makes his way he drops his hat. Rushing to pick it up,
he inadvertently kicks it across the floor. EVERYONE in the courtroom begins
to laugh. The JUDGE stomps the gavel. FLEET gives the prosecuting attorney
a despairing glance. KNOWLTON motions with his head that he should keep
moving, ignore the hat, and carry on. FLEET, one hand on the Bible, salutes
the flag with military stiffness and takes the stand.*

Direct-examination.

KNOWLTON: You're an assistant to the Marshal
in the city of old Fall River
on the day the crime took place
and a city was left to shiver.

FLEET: Yes I am, in the city of Fall River.

KNOWLTON: As soon as you had arrived
you quizzed Miss Borden of the death
and did she give up the truth
spilled her secrets in one breath?

FLEET: I interrogated Lizzie Borden
as soon as I arrived
and of her trip to the barn
I could tell that she had lied,
she said she was in the loft
her response was left of snide
for twenty minutes she had stayed
in the barn while her father died,

and of her mother I did probe
which she had rudely replied
she's no mother of mine, dear Sir,
I was a child when my mother died.

KNOWLTON: Now let us speak of your cursory tour
to the cellar where the axe was found
which Officer Mullaly had on display
in the basement deep underground.

FLEET: Mullaly showed me to a dusty box
where I found a hatchet head
laying with a thick coat of ash
the murder weapon it may be said.

KNOWLTON: A piece of handle was broken off
and protruded from the steel
would you say the break was fresh
can we say that is how you feel?

FLEET: The handle I did not find
in the box it did not dwell
a piece was severed at the head

but of the handle, I cannot tell
it looked freshly broken, Sir
of foul play it sure did smell.

KNOWLTON *returns to his desk, while* JENNINGS *gets up asking a question as he approaches* FLEET.

Cross-examination.

JENNINGS: Now, Mr. Fleet—
                of all the inquires we ask today
                rummaging of the barn and dress
                the search of closets and for blood
                the truth here you must confess,
                tell us what you have uncovered
                the products of your success.

FLEET: Counselor now, I do concede
                I appear to be full of bull
                but on the her clothes we found no blood
                on cotton, silk or wool
                and of the handle I saw none
                an axe head in the box was all
                but searches are not my forte'
                unlike a barroom brawl.

JENNINGS: From your testimony we conclude
                you found no proof at all
                no blood on axe or dress
                any evidence you can't recall,
                but if we have a tavern row
                we can simply give you a call?

FLEET: That's correct, and in response
                we will not impede or stall
                when it comes to murder now
                I'm afraid it is our pitfall,
                but if you speak of outings
                like picnics or a barbecue
                we'll be there with forks and spoons
                but a murder we just can't do.

JENNINGS: Of this witness I am through.

JUDGE: Mr. Knowlton, your next witness, please.

KNOWLTON: Yes, Your Honor, I would like to call
              my next witness to the galley
              who will tell us all he knows
              one Officer Michael Mullaly.

MULLALY is sworn in. He takes the stand and is ready to be questioned. He appears to be very competent and comes off as being creditable.

Direct-examination.

KNOWLTON: We appeal to the officer
              with veracity for the facts
              of all he knew and had discovered
              about the box with the broken axe.

MULLALY: With the maid I went to the cellar
              where two axes she did acquire
              the two displayed here in court
              and the head with ash and mire.

KNOWLTON: Did you speak with Miss Lizzie
              and unearth any deep concern
              whether it was a dastardly burglar
              of this crime, what did you learn?

MULLALY: The Marshal had promptly sent me
              to inquire and explore
              from the dead man's grieving child
              what she knew or had in store,

              she declared that her father
              had a watch and some dough,
              a wallet with some money
              and a gold ring on his toe...
              I mean his on his finger...
              and that nothing was gone or taken
              as far she could tell or show.

KNOWLTON: No more questions.

ANDREW JENNINGS stands and addresses MULLALY.

Cross-examination.

JENNINGS: Now, Officer Mullaly,
              you were there to do a search

and found a handle in a box
was it made of oak or birch?

MULLALY: To that I cannot say, dear Sir,
            a woodsman I am not
            when in the cellar we all went
            since I thought it worth a shot,
            when we opened the dusty box
            there was a splintered axe
            with a fractured piece of wood
            from much too many whacks.

JENNINGS: While you were there, can you describe
            what else it was you found
            in the box that held the axe
            any secrets which you unbound,
            since Marshal Fleet says it's not true
            no handle, as you proclaim
            of this statement you both tell
            are you a liar or is he to blame?

MULLALY: Mr. Fleet did have the wood
            to that I will swear
            where it went since that day
            I can't tell why it's not there,

            after all, we are just police
            most times we're not quite sure
            and to this misdeed we tried and tried
            yet could not find a cure,

            but, if you have a dire need
            and I'm sure we all agree
            that we are very skillful, Sir,
            take a cat down from a tree,

            and when it comes to a dire crime
            it's at best misbegotten
            and though this is not Denmark, Sir,
            somethin' sure as hell smells rotten.

JENNINGS turns and addresses the counsel for the prosecution.

JENNINGS: Mr. Knowlton, I ask you now
            the handle can you produce

	is it in your possession, Sir,
	to that can we deduce?

KNOWLTON:	To respond to what you speak
	I haven't got a clue
	to where it is, or where it's gone
	to me this talk's all new.

JENNINGS:	Fine, Officer Mullaly,
	I have no more
	in the way of questions
	I concede the floor.

JENNINGS leaves and KNOWLTON stands and approaches the JUDGE.

KNOWLTON:	Your Honor, if it pleases the court
	and with no further procrastination
	we call the physician of postmortem
	so we can engage him in confabulation.

JUDGE:	Very well, counselor,
	call your next witness,
	without any hesitation.

KNOWLTON:	I call upon Doctor William Dolan
	to emerge and face the court
	so we can question what he knows
	what evidence he does support,
	and of the axe found in the box
	that she did use to kill
	we will prove it as the blade
	that caused the blood to spill,
	and of that hatchet we will show
	like an iceberg through a hull
	it was the crushing instrument
	buried in the victim's skull.

As HOSEA KNOWLTON makes his commencement speech, DR. WILLIAM DOLAN is sworn in and takes the stand.

Direct-examination.

KNOWLTON:	Now, Doctor—
	judging by the wounds

on Mr. Andrew Borden's head,
the slashes left behind
beneath and within the red
could it have been a woman
not a man who caused all the dread
an axe with ordinary strength
could a female have embed?

DR. DOLAN: It could have been a woman
with little strength or muscle
who swung the axe with skill and ease
and inconsequential bustle,
and from the unsuspecting victims
there would have been little rustle
and chopped up those two victims
with little fuss, or tussle.

KNOWLTON: Can you fix the precise moment
Mr. Borden could have died
was it long or short time after
the demise of his old bride?

DR. DOLAN: In my examination and study
of the blood and it's flow
Andrew Borden's oozed out freely
Abby Borden did quite slow,

it was more than an hour
more than two, I cannot say
between the time Abby passed
and Andrew's life was swept away.

KNOWLTON: Can you tell us how you arrived
at the time line of the death
when Mrs. Borden passed away
and Mr. Borden lost his breath?

DR. DOLAN: Of breakfast which was eaten
with digestion still in play
in both the victims stomachs
and with confidence I can weight
the degree of decomposition
the food I did survey.

KNOWLTON: Now, of splatter and of blood

I'm sure you can't ignore
of shower, froth, and sprinkle
on the wall, ceiling, floor.

In your forensic endeavor
speak of blood you did find
on the axe with the ash
was there proof left behind?

DR. DOLAN: Both sides of the hatchet
contained spots that were rusty
though they first appear suspicious
as for blood they weren't trusty,
with only wet oxidation
otherwise I'd call it dusty
if you like to give it tenure
also smelly, soiled and musty.

KNOWLTON: Now we have here some axes
we'll call them Exhibit A and B
have you examined these weapons
to the ultimate degree,

did you find human hair
on the handles or blade
and on the blue dress
any blood that could aid
to solve this dastardly crime
can any evidence be made?

DR. DOLAN: I have tested all the axes
and found one single hair
on the blade of a hatchet
and with you I can share,

it was not at all crucial
though it may raise a single brow
the lone hair that I discovered
grew out of a cow,

and as for the blue dress
it was also a dud
after clinical studies
I discovered no blood.

KNOWLTON: Thank you, Doctor Dolan,
if it please the court, I rest.

KNOWLTON returns to his station at the prosecution desk while JENNINGS walks over to DR. DOLAN. As both men pass one another their elbows brush.

Cross-examination.

JENNINGS: Doctor Dolan—
if I understand
a visit to the Bordens
was not really your plan,
you were just making rounds
when your involvement began?

DR. DOLAN: I was driving to see a patient
it was very close to noon
when I went into the Borden House
what I found would make you swoon.

ANDREW JENNINGS turns and faces the JURY.

JENNINGS: Now, Doctor Dolan—
Lizzie Borden took an axe
gave her father forty whacks
when she saw what she had done
she gave her mother forty-one—
is that what you have heard?

DR. DOLAN: If Lizzie Borden took an axe
it's not for me to say
but of the numbers you declare
of the truth it does betray,
Mrs. Borden received nineteen whacks
but that was not to be outdone
when the attacker saw what they did
the old chap earned ten plus one.

JENNINGS: As we can see they got it wrong
the details and the facts
thus, we are here to prove today
Lizzie innocent of these attacks,
now, you removed the victims beans
was it accomplished with approval

did you try and get permission
from the family for removal?

DR. DOLAN: I don't remember, but I can say
we just didn't have the time
it was urgent to investigate
the specifics to this crime,
so, OFF WITH HIS HEAD, was the call
the recommendation was partially mine.

JENNINGS: Do you actually claim dispensation
when you detached the head from the spine?

DR. DOLAN: I did not require anyone's consent
the daughters did not know
when I severed both their heads
in a surgical cameo,
into a box they went, plop
and to my office they did go
where I studied them more carefully
how the hatchet took it's blow.

JENNINGS: Did you not make up plaster casts
of the heads for the court's display
and they are here this very while
to testify for us today?

DR. DOLAN continues his medical rendition. His voice slows and deepens. His eyes narrow, his head oscillates, protruding at times like an inquisitive turtle, as he eyes the JURY. He speaks direct and candidly, lethargically, almost lackadaisical, as if bored by the details. LIZZIE BORDEN sits quietly, her head in her hands. She displays explicit grief.

DR. DOLAN: Yes, first the heads went into a vat
let them simmer, the flame real low
then the fire began to blaze
as the fire began to grow,
they didn't seem to mind
or if they did, it didn't show,

in a broth of anthropoid fat
off came all the droopy skin
hair, muscle, cartilage, warts
cheeks, ears, and chin,
after removing all limber flesh

eyes, nose, lips, and smile
the Borden crowns where predisposed
as witnesses in this trial.

JENNINGS: Yes... interesting observation—
but let's talk of splatter
of blood on the wall
of blood on the doors
of blood which did fall,
on the assailant and his person
and how the killer did fair
the salvo of sprinkles
upon his clothes and his hair.

DR. DOLAN: There was blood, leaks and drippings
splattered all over the sitting room
on the floor, bed and walls
on the ceiling, roof and moon,
Mr. Borden's was quite red
Abby Borden, a parched maroon.
I'd say Abby was killed much sooner
after nine but before noon.

JENNINGS: Let's talk of flying hatchets
the width and the depth
made into the skull
of Mr. Borden as he slept,
when the butcher did gain access
the assassin which he met.

DR. DOLAN: Of the wounds, there were many
they were vicious, wide, and deep
by a hatchet which inflicted
the contusions in his sleep,

one blow surgically severed
the man's eyeball in two
like a barber's keen honed razor
one blow of quite a few.

JENNINGS: And the girth of the blade
was it six, four, or two.
of the flesh it did mince
of the tissue it did chew?

DR. DOLAN: One was less than an inch
               with the longest about five
               of those which I measured
               no one could survive.

JENNINGS: How long was the blade
               of the instrument that was used
               of the cleaver, axe, or hatchet
               and the injuries suffused?

DR. DOLAN: I would say three and half inches
               was the instrument that was used
               to lacerate the arteries
               and blood vessels that were oozed,
               I couldn't quite believe
               the way these old folks were abused
               when I entered the bloody house
               I was not one bit amused.

JENNINGS: I have nothing further to add
               in my defense of the accused.

*JENNINGS returns to his station at his desk, while KNOWLTON quickly rises
and approaches DR. DOLAN yet once more for a re-direct.*

Re-direct-examination.

KNOWLTON: Well, we have spoken of the number
               of blows which were dispatched
               the scope, angle, and the width
               of the wounds and life it snatched
               do you agree?

DR. DOLAN: One cut through the forehead
               another shaved off his nose
               abrasions to his cheeks were many
               casting a horror in repose,

               it was really quite the sight
               and for those who really care
               the man was quite right rich
               but his millions he would not share.

KNOWLTON: And that's why we are here today
               and to the sweat which kept you busy

now let us prove to the jurors here
the sins of one called Lizzie,

but to do this I do regret
Andrew Borden must testify
can someone summon him to court
just his head would need apply.

DOCTOR WILLIAM DOLAN stands proud, with a pleased and sinister smile. He procures a dusty fruit box on the floor behind him. He holds it up above his shoulders and moves it from left to right so everyone could see. Placing it on a small table by the side of the stand he rubs his hands together and displays them to the court, fingers spread and wiggling. He looks up one jacket sleeve, then the other, revealing the fact that he hides nothing. He unbuttons his coat and spreads it open, turning left to right displaying the silk lining. Demonstrating that he conceals nothing, he turns his pockets inside out. Now he is ready. He carefully removes the flimsy wood slat lid for the box and hands it to the BAILIFF who acts as his jovial assistant. The BAILIFF bows gracefully, and like a ballerina whirling on her toes, with ankles tightly crossed, he takes miniature steps and dances away. Slowly, as if placing his hands into a box of glutinous cement, he inserts his spread fingers and slowly pulls out the skull of Andrew Jackson Borden, as if he had just finalized a conjuring trick, pulled the rabbit out of his hat. The SPECTATORS stand, applaud, and cheer with astonishing enthusiasm. As the ovation continues LIZZIE BORDEN, in a woozy sway, lowers her head and buries it in her hands.

LIZZIE stands. The light in the room fades to dark with the only illumination on LIZZIE's face. One can hear the gavel banging. The SPECTATORS grow silent. LIZZIE now looks up at the light and begs.

LIZZIE: The bird cries bloody murder
I can hear him in my breast,
as the halberd severs further
a fathers love gone to rest.

When will this all stop
this raping of my soul,
efface this damning spot
thus pneuma black as coal.
Now they display poor Father
in shameful and heinous slander,
strip me of divine ardor
leaving desire to beg and pander.

Why can't they just discern

innocence and guilt, the same,
the culpable right of ice to burn
like the honor in the Borden name.

While this stony skull can't speak
of the love we had to share,
the avalanche of tears on cheek
recite an Iscariotic prayer.

And as June suckles on summer's breast
and the nightingale begins to sing,
I wish the courage to confess
Father's love to nurse and cling.

But they refuse to understand
the sonnets in my heart,
instead conspire, plot and plan
to tear our strength apart.

And ignore the mournful hymn
Philomela's sacred tongue,
as the Nightingale confirms the sin
in the poem which she has sung.

And just because my love is mute
for this Escort and his wife,
that I loved him there's no dispute
yet I'm left to fight for life.

Now they chase away the swallow
and conspire with a severed head,
and serve it up quite hollow
the consecration of the dead.

But I'll be strong and forceful
you know I love you Papa,
and I'll remain resourceful
for our love was pure and proper.
One can't burst a daughter's emotion
though they say it does not exist,
the solitude of a love's devotion
for which she does enlist.

So why would I do such a thing
to snuff out that which I love,

and not to hear the bird and sing
the nightingale above.

LIZZIE BORDEN exhibits a stiff upper lip, sits back down in her chair, and makes a valiant attempt to continue to endure DR. DOLAN's testimony, the lights in the room brighten.

KNOWLTON: Excellent presentation, Doctor—
              now, how an axe could have fit
              can you proceed on with the show
              with the holes made by the blow
              of the axe with a handle
              which was lost a long time ago?

JENNINGS: *(Interrupts.)* Assuming it was an axe.
              used by the foe.

DR. DOLAN: How would you like to begin
              above the nose or above the chin?

KNOWLTON hands DR. DOLAN the handless axe head. DOLAN strokes it with a smile as if given a valued gift.

KNOWLTON: Demonstrate how the axe did fit
              by prodding the instrument into the hole
              here with the gap, there at the split
              where the whacks did take their toll.

WILLIAM DOLAN demonstrates how the handless axe fit the wounds. He thrusts the axe head into one wound in the skull and carefully slides it into others. Every time he does he scans the room, arches his eyebrows, and smiles.

DR. DOLAN: As you can see this hole is quite large
              it swallows the iron when I push and slide
              but here the axe is hard to lodge
              yet through the eye the hatchet did glide.

KNOWLTON: Now would you say, can you indicate
              that it could be the tool
              that was used in the Borden crime
              would that be your truthful rule?

DR. DOLAN: I would say that's the device
              that made that huge crater
              upon the man's mangled face
              by a traitor or hater,

and when the carotid artery
was severed by the axe a new
death would be almost instant
perhaps a second, three, or two,
before the soul left the body
and demise indeed ensue.

KNOWLTON: *(To the JUDGE.)*
              I rest the floor, I am through.

JUDGE: We will break, a well earned recess
              from this case which has begun
              Bailiff, dismiss the jurors
              we will continue after one.

The JUDGE brings down the gavel, once. EVERYONE in the courtroom stands as he walks out. The scene goes dark, with the only light concentrated on the card table where DARROW challenges BRYAN's hand.

DARROW: My, my, that was quite the testimony.
BRYAN: Damning.
DARROW: To?
BRYAN: The defense—who do you think? Now you have made the challenge.
  Are you going to show your cards?

Unsure, DARROW studies his cards closely. BRYAN, excited and eager about his hand can't wait and spreads his cards on the table.

BRYAN: Three ladies and two knaves.
DARROW: *(Not showing his cards, throws them down.)* Fold!
BRYAN: *(Reaching for the match sticks.)* God bless the doctor.
DARROW: Damn Dolan.
BRYAN: *(Gets up from his chair, puts on his coat.)* His testimony alone may
  be enough to convict.
DARROW: You may be right... but not correct.

WILLIAM JENNINGS BRYAN starts out of the room.

DARROW: Not so quick. *(Chasing after BRYAN as he leaves the courtroom.)*
  Most of the evidence proved nothing. No blood on Liz or her dress—no
  blood on the handless axe or any other axe.

DARROW and BRYAN exit.

BLACKOUT

ACT II
Scene Five

As the lights come up, DARROW and BRYAN are standing together on the dock at the waterfront, which is just down the street from the court house. DARROW tries to catch his breath as he attempts to light a cigarette. BRYAN looks out to sea, looking optimistic and snub. DARROW shows him his pack of cigarettes, offering him one. BRYAN waves him off.

BRYAN: Come now, Clarence. That axe head fit into the wounds perfectly.

DARROW: Proves nothing. Most hatchets that size would fit those wounds. It's a very common implement. Everyone has one in their basement or kitchen. Every carpenter carries one. The prosecution never proved that it was the actual instrument. And what of the handle?

BRYAN: Ah, Clarence. The handle is insignificant. You are not listening to the spirit of performance.

DARROW: Performance?

BRYAN: If your evidence is weak, your presentation must overwhelm— you must give the audience a lively and spirited performance.

DARROW: With that evidence. Intimidating the defendant and shocking the jurors with the victim's skull. You call that evidence.

BRYAN: Statutory damage.

DARROW: It will not work.

BRYAN: I beg to disagree, my dear man. Think, the law of impartiality. Though you may think the prosecution will not prove the handless hatchet as the weapon that committed the killings, the defense will not prove, unequivocally, that it was not. That my good man may be all that's needed.

DARROW: Lack of absolute proof favors the defense and the element of doubt. If there is doubt, the jury must stand down and relay a verdict of not guilty.

BRYAN: Not if the performance is overwhelming, the component of un-certainty is obscured. All one need do is convince a simple jury—no, let me rephrase that, entertain a simple jury, derail their sensibilities, shock their consternation, and convince them that this appalling crime needs a villain, and we have only one. Lizzie Borden. And if that is what is needed to achieve justice, then I am glad to see it.

DARROW: I see you have learned much from me. But Lizzie Borden? Guilty?

BRYAN: Precisely. Guilty as sin.

DARROW: An axe- wielding woman?

BRYAN: Absolutely.

DARROW: You forget. The accused is the victim's daughter. Do you really believe that twelve men will convict a woman to hang?

BRYAN: I certainly do.

DARROW: Unlikely.

BRYAN: Ask your Greek friend. Are not his mythological stories ones you subscribe to? Did not his Electra try to kill her father Aegisthus? Well that is how it is with Lizzie Borden. A Victorian Electra.

DARROW: Stepfather, Bryan, stepfather. Electra did not try to kill her father. Aegisthus was her stepfather. Abby was Liz's stepmother. You have the Bordens and Aegisthus mixed up.

BRYAN: Murder is murder. Does not matter what the relationship. The taking of a human life is a transgression upon God.

DARROW takes possession of a fishing rod wedged between two whale oil barrels, and casts the line and empty hook into the bay.

DARROW: I thought we placed God back into His pencil box.

BRYAN: Funny thing about Lizzie Borden. My Mary also loves to go fishing. She loves the quiet, the rustling of the stream, the trees. Ah! The trees—especially in the autumn—the color and the scent of crisp woodland air. God, Illinois is beautiful in the autumn. You know, Clarence, that Scopes Trial knocked a few years out of me. I remember sitting at home a day later, when suddenly you called and invited me on this, this... well, what can I call it—an allegorical excursion?

DARROW: Well, I'm just grateful you have no hard feelings about that Scopes trial. I knew all you needed was some time to get away, some entertainment.

BRYAN: The trial of Lizzie Borden, a courtroom—you call that entertainment.

DARROW: Sure. Lizzie Borden's trial was the most riveting, engaging play I have ever witnessed.

BRYAN: Still, it cannot compare to a day of fishing back home on Lake Carlyle—my wife by my side. Have you ever met my wife Mary, Clarence? *(BRYAN doesn't give DARROW a chance to reply.)* Smart woman, my Mary—good lawyer—brilliant speech-writer.

DARROW: Sure, sure, I have spoken with her many times.

BRYAN: *(Picking up a few stones, he tosses them into the water.)* Ah, Mary, I wish you were here. You could teach the people of this time period a thing or two.

DARROW: Do you think she would find Lizzie Borden guilty?

BRYAN: *(Chuckling.)* I hate to admit it, but I dare add that she would probably volunteer to represent her free of charge.

DARROW: She probably would, at that.

BRYAN: You know, this harbor would be beautiful, if not for all these damn old ships.

DARROW: Whalers. They are not the most immaculate vessels, but they built this city.

BRYAN: There must me two hundred barrels stacked on this dock. All this whale oil. I swear everyone of them is oozing the pinguidity which is humanity. This is a strange town. I have never seen so many foreigners and in one place. Hate to see what this place will look like in our day.

DARROW: Even by this time whaling was on the decline, you know. The petroleum industry has a harpoon through its heart. Look up at the city. Tell me, what do you see?

BRYAN: Church steeples, fishing sheds, a cooper's shop.

DARROW: No, further on.

BRYAN: Why yes, the city proper.

DARROW: No, Bryan, mills. Cotton mills. This once whaling giant is at the peak of industrial transformation. It's a workingman's town.

BRYAN: *(Nodding.)* So it is.

DARROW: You're not in Dayton, Tennessee. This is the industrial Northeast. Land of men and monkeys, where the Bible is hidden in your breast pocket and not under your arm—and in most cases, not at all. Where a girl, charged with patricide can receive a fair trial.

BRYAN: Perhaps too fair.

DARROW: That is why I always fight for the hapless, the misunderstood.

BRYAN: And that explains why you are defending a rich Victorian woman?

DARROW: Well, she is misunderstood. You've got to give her that. In this case I have little choice but to defend her. Unless, you want to defend her and I will fight for the state to have her hung.

BRYAN: Not on your life. I will get it done.

DARROW: *(Shaking his head and smiling.)* I thought so.

BRYAN: She killed her father, Clarence—an upright citizen, man of principle, a financial cornerstone in the community. If not for people like Andrew Jackson Borden building towns like this, where would the common folk be? How would they live?

DARROW: People like Borden do not build them alone. Towns like New Bedford, Fall River, and countless others across this country were built by hard working, and sometimes, wretched, impoverished individuals. Not solely by aristocratic bankers such as Mr. Borden. The wheel would never turn without its spokes, Bryan. Remember that.

BRYAN: Most of these new age settlers are still better off here than in their own countries.

DARROW: Does not mean you don't pay them a fair wage?

BRYAN throws his hands in the air and walks away, trying to avoid further conversation on the matter. There's a long pause of silence.

BRYAN: Look way over there, to the south. They are building a new mill. There's growth, enterprise—takes money, Clarence, money. And people like Andrew Borden.

DARROW: *(Ignoring BRYAN, he removes his hat and wipes his face with a handkerchief.)* It looks like it's turning into a hot one.

BRYAN: *(Staring south, proudly clenching his jacket lapels.)* Ah... give me your tired, your poor, your huddled masses yearning to breathe free, send me these, the homeless and I will lift my lamp beside the golden door.

DARROW: Yes, give me your tired and your poor and we will keep them that way, we will huddle them in mill houses, coerce them to return their hard earned pay in our mill stores, breathe our bad air...

BRYAN: Not so! Ask any one of them if they are not happy to have a job. To be taken care of. Ask any one of them if entering that golden door was not a prudent choice.

DARROW: In many cases that golden door is a snare, attached to a cage.

BRYAN: *(Having his proud moment spoiled.)* Let us agree to disagree and talk of something else?

DARROW removes a half spent cigarette from his mouth and flicks it into the bay. He places the fishing rod back where he had found it.

DARROW: Very well. The cross examination of Doctor Seabury Bowen, the family doctor—let's talk about that.

BRYAN: Yes go on, what about it?

DARROW: I think the prosecution's case lost some ground with the morphine testimony, don't you?

BRYAN: How so?

DARROW: Liz must have been an impassive corpse in the early days after the crime. He practically had a syringe strapped to her arm.

BRYAN: I don't see that summarization to be applicable. Lizzie Borden still carries her condescending soulless manner to this very day.

DARROW: The fact that she appeared insensitive days after the crime or uncaring—the drug probably accounted for much of that behavior.

BRYAN: She's a cool killer. She truly believes, that she can get away with it, thus the narcissistic heartlessness.

DARROW: I think you have been reading the Globe again.

BRYAN: I don't need a newspaper to tell me what I have studied about this case. Or do you think I don't come prepared?

DARROW: I'm sure you do. So tell me. What was the purpose of having the family physician testify against her?

BRYAN: Several. He was called to testify to the dress worn the morning of the crime—that it was not the one she handed in as State evidence, not a dark blue dress, but a light blue, a drab color.

DARROW: Let us stay with the doctor and the dress. You must admit that the old doctor became somewhat of a hostile witness for the prosecution.

BRYAN: Yes, I know, I know.

DARROW: Knowlton tried his best to get the good doctor to testify to the description of the dress Lizzie was wearing the morning of the murders. Bowen made tracks around him. He never really answered the question to the satisfaction of the court. That hurt the prosecution's case.

BRYAN: Bowen appeared to go out of his way to be vague about the dress.

DARROW: I wouldn't go that far. After all, he described the dress as drab, indefinite, a morning calico dress—a common dress.

BRYAN: They asked him about the color, the color. He refused to choose and insisted on being ambiguous.

DARROW: I thought the response evident. He said there was no color to it. If I remember correctly, his exact words were, "I don't remember distinctly anything about the color." They wanted him to describe the dress that was burnt up in the kitchen stove and he wouldn't do it.

BRYAN: I suppose. One thing is for certain, the dress Lizzie Borden gave the court is not one she wore early morning August 4th, 1892. That much is obvious.

DARROW: Most men are not fashion minded as you, Bryan. I dare say, some only look beyond what a women is wearing. Their eyes are not looking at it but through it.

BRYAN: That is your presumed assessment to male's preoccupation when it comes to women, is it?

DARROW: Well, what did your wife have on the last time you spoke to her?

BRYAN: To tell you the truth, I couldn't tell you what my wife was wearing the last time we spoke.

DARROW: Well then, you can see the good doctor's dilemma.

BRYAN: But, I remember her face, her smile, warm, gentle, caring.

DARROW: But not what she was wearing!

BRYAN: In any event, Adelaide Churchill testified that the dress in Knowlton's possession was not the dress Lizzie was wearing the morning of the crime. She gave a detailed description of what it looked like. And the dress here today is not the dress worn. Then there was the maid's description.

DARROW: You believe Churchill?

BRYAN: You have reason why I should not?

DARROW: On the stand she could not describe the dress all the other women had on that day, including Bridget, Alice Russell, and the Doctor's wife.

BRYAN: Your point...

DARROW: Furthermore, the doctor's wife testified she was the one fanning Liz, stood beside her, and never saw a drop of blood on the her."

BRYAN: Yes, yes, I know. Let me think... And I wish you would stop calling her Liz.

DARROW: What we have here is the modus operandi for a speedy trial. The prosecution needs the blood evidence, or at the very least, proof that one of the hatchets they have is the murder weapon.

BRYAN: And they will have it.

DARROW: How?

BRYAN: The handless axe is the weapon.

DARROW: Come now, Bryan, I don't think even the State believes that. Where's the handle, where's the blood?

BRYAN: She killed her parents with that hatchet, washed it, broke the handle off, and destroyed it in the kitchen stove. Then she took the axe head and hid it in a box in the cellar.

DARROW: Whether anyone believes that or not will come out in the wash at the end of this trial. The true crux to the entire prosecution is contingent on a handful of circumstantial confirmations, as the State sees it, most of it resting on the unequivocal assertion that Liz lied.

BRYAN: Her name is Lizzie, and which she did lie. She lied about the note Abby received, about trying to purchase prussic acid, about the dress she wore, and her whereabouts at the time her father was killed, about searching for tin, for lead, for iron, and God knows what else.

DARROW: I concede. She possessed the opportunity and the motive. But nothing of what you just mentioned applies.

BRYAN: So you agree she had motive? Your convictions and wisdom are starting to filter through, are they?

DARROW: On the contrary. *(Lights another cigarette.)* I am not debating that she is innocent—just that she is not guilty.

BRYAN: Bah!

DARROW: It's like you said, Bryan. It's all about the performance.

There's a long pause of silence, as DARROW and BRYAN take in the invigorating salty air and admire the New Bedford harbor.

BRYAN: You know, this is really a lovely harbor, if not for these rotting, worm-eaten vessels—to say little of the odor of decomposing fish. Fairhaven across the way is quite beautiful—green with tiny carpet lawns, neat little homes, spotted with red maples and weeping willows—a white steeple on a lonely church.

DARROW: In many respects, this is the real America. Colonists first settled this country less than forty miles from here. Pilgrims, I think they called them.

BRYAN: *(BRYAN shakes his head at DARROW's little joke.)* It reminds me of a poem I once read. It went... ah?

Plunging ships armed with net
ambush the adolescent sun
and in the southern horizon,
they take to black rippled waters
over the naked of the bay
where vagabond gulls cry
at the anchors they weigh.

With cloud piercing bows
their timber snouts punch
an angry puffing swell
marching with the waves
to the buoy, to the bell.

And from a paramour shore
which dissolves and retreats
wheels the weeping hull of the Laura B
with line and rope, boom and cloth
she rides high and proud
pointing south and north.

And trailing behind is the Maria Fatima
with the Christina May
the Mary Moore
and the Salty Jay,
while their transoms fade
to the glow of the day
to the Flemish Cap
to Georgia by the banks
through the foam and brine
hoping they'll return
to their families in time.
Weathered faced wives
pace docks and piers
where their hearts fade pale
in the white of their years.

Where boats of wood, batten and plank
carry men of steel, and no particular rank
who fish with their hearts
a great distance from land
with a compass and chart
and by their God's right hand.

DARROW: Eloquent, Bryan. I didn't realize you had it in you.

BRYAN: Comes from trying to memorize speeches, you know. It's called "The Weeping Hull of the Laura B." The meter is off, and I have forgotten a few stanzas and rhymes, but looking out to sea here, you get the picture.

DARROW: We sure do.

There is a long pause as DARROW and BRYAN stare out to the bay.

BRYAN: I want Eli Bence to testify at trial.

DARROW: You can't have Bence.

BRYAN: I want Eli Bence on the stand. His testimony is too worthwhile to be omitted.

DARROW: Bence did not appear in court at the original trial... he was excluded.

BRYAN: That was a miscalculation.

DARROW: He was a witness for the prosecution. It was the State's team who chose not to call him.

BRYAN: I would like to change that.

DARROW: Have you thought this through carefully, Bryan? There had to be good reason why he was not called as a witness.

BRYAN: I thought his inquest testimony incontrovertible.

DARROW: *(Ignoring BRYAN's reply.)* And it usually has to do with character —rectitude. They must have found damaging character flaws in Bence— moral stature, ill repute, perhaps he was lying. There had to be good reason why he was not allowed to complete his testimony.

BRYAN: Well, he will this time. Are you going to agree or not?

DARROW: *(Smiling and shaking his head.)* The trial should be starting shortly. It's best we start back.

BRYAN: Yes, it's best.

DARROW and BRYAN walk up the cobble blanketed road to the courthouse on the hill.

DARROW: *(His arm around BRYAN's shoulder.)* You know, Bryan, you could win this poker game. After all you are ahead.

BRYAN: You think I don't know that?

DARROW: Four out of seven hands. All you need do is win one more and Lizzie Borden hangs. Do you really want Bence on the stand?

BRYAN: Eli Bence will testify.

CURTAIN

ACT III
Scene One

Back at the courtroom the trial resumes. DARROW and BRYAN take their places at the rear of the room. A light shines only upon the card table and the two men. After dealing from the deck, DARROW spreads his cards, studies them, and immediately looks up at the portrait over BRYAN's head, surveying BRYAN's hand from the reflection in the glass. The lights suddenly come on and the room is instantly illuminated. The JUDGE enters. EVERYONE in the courtroom stands. As is now common, they break into cheers and enthusiastic applause, yet once again. Banging his gavel everyone sits, the room goes silent, and the trial of Lizzie Borden continues.

JUDGE: *(Banging gavel.)*
              Come to order, come to order,
              counsel take your places
              let's return to the Borden slaughter
              where smiles cannot find faces.

              Now, Mr. Jennings, you may call
              the next witness to the floor
              ask him questions big and small
              interrogate him to the core.

ANDREW JENNINGS leaves his desk and approaches the bench.

JENNINGS: I call for Thomas Barlow
              and another townie
              please approach the stand
              and bring your friend Brownie.

THOMAS BARLOW and EVERETT BROWN approach the stand together. They punch at each other, jousting, and pushing until they take their places at the rail. They look to be around sixteen years of age, full of vim and vinegar. JENNINGS waits for them to cease their horseplay. The BAILIFF comes over and extends the Bible. BARLOW places his hand on it and BROWN places his hand over BARLOW's. After they are sworn the BAILIFF pulls the book away rolls his eyes and shakes his head, and quickly meanders away.

Direct-examination.

JENNINGS: Your name is Everett Brown
                    and you are Thomas Barlow
                    tell the court where you live
                    and any facts we can follow.

BROWN: I live at 117 Third Street
                    with my mum and my dad.

BARLOW: I live up on Lyon
                    where it's not really bad.

JENNINGS: Now tell us, Mr. Barlow,
                    did you go down to the scene
                    where there was a social gathering
                    and what time did it seem?

BARLOW: We trudged along Third Street
                    from Morgan down to Second
                    with my friend Everett Brown
                    when to the Borden's he did beckon.

                    I left the house, at 11 a.m.
                    of the clock and what it said
                    to Brownie's who lived down the block
                    then to the house of the slain and dead.

BROWN: We prowled into the Borden yard
                    where the murders were said and done
                    but we were barred from the house
                    left to bake out in the sun.

JENNINGS: And when you arrived
                    what did you discover or find
                    at the address you mention
                    can you please search your mind?

BROWN: Sawyer stood at the door
            with that grimace and scowl.

BARLOW: It became quite a chore
            he had eyes like an owl.

BROWN: I said—
            "Hey bud, let us inside"

BARLOW: "We can help solve this misdeed"

BROWN: No matter how hard, we tried and tried

BARLOW: He wouldn't give in or concede.

JENNINGS: Now, when you first got there—
            did you see any people
            around the house or the yard
            and while you were there,
            did you find it that hard
            to enter the property
            with any resolve or regard?

BARLOW: When we arrived I did view
            the police and some fuzz.

BROWN: Fleet and Doherty dressed in blue
            the police were in a buzz.

BARLOW: And the lawn was swarming
            with women and gents.

BROWN: A crowd was forming
            over the day's long events.

BARLOW: And we looked into the house
            to gather some blood and some gore
            in the window we did browse
            since they would not let us in the door.

JENNINGS: Now tell the court—
            when you approached Charlie Sawyer
            and were unsuccessful at gaining entry
            what did you do, where did you go
            when refused access by the sentry?

BROWN: We went over to the barn
                and tried to open the door
                we slipped the lock and pulled the latch
                while the police we did ignore,

                we stood inside, somewhat in fear
                of going up the loft ahead
                I dared Barlow to lead the way
                he spoke of alarm and dread
                that an axe may fall from the sky
                and hit him on the head,

                but we found our courage
                and I led the way
                to the loft window above
                and the straw and the hay
                where we stayed for five minutes
                in the attic to survey.

JENNINGS: Where did you go after the barn
                the visit that you made that day?

BROWN: We went to the door
                and tried to peek in
                but Sawyer was keen
                he just stood there with a grin,
                until Officer Fleet
                put us out on the street
                to the sadness of our chagrin.

JENNINGS: Thank you, Mr. Brown, Mr. Barlow,
                Mr. Knowlton, you may go
                to where I have been.

Cross-examination.

KNOWLTON: Good morning, Mr. Barlow...
                good morning, Mr. Brown...
                let's get to the meat
                let's feed the hound,
                now was the barn door locked
                with a staple or nail
                and gaining access inside
                did you achieve without fail?

BROWN: Tommy Barlow tried the door
           and opened it without care
           he said, "Let's go inside
           there maybe someone in there"
           that if the killer may be hiding
           beneath the hay we could snare.

KNOWLTON: And as for you, Mr. Barlow,
           can you please tell the court
           what you do for a living
           what's your bio in short?

BARLOW: I work at Shannon's poolroom
           and set up the balls from within
           but it's not the sort of pool
           where you can go for a swim
           it's where men hit a ball
           with a cue and a spin.

KNOWLTON: That's all very interesting
           you have a job that's a jewel
           but when you went into the barn
           where you say it was cool
           on the hottest day of the year
           do you think I'm a fool?

BARLOW: Whether you are or you're not
           to say would be cruel.

KNOWLTON: Don't be coy, Mr. Barlow,
           you're a man not a mule
           just because I'm a lawyer—
           and you have no school
           I can see that your story
           is a truth without fuel,

           now you went into the loft
           where the killer may be hiding
           did you go to the hay
           is that the story you're providing?

BARLOW: We went up into the loft
           for the killer to find
           where we turned over hay
           looked underneath and behind

to the loft window we looked
for the villain or swine
where footprints we left
in the dust and the grime.

KNOWLTON: Now—
testimony from the police
of the loft and the barn
the story police told
their attestation and their yarn,

that the dust in the loft
was found undisturbed
that no one had been there
not even a bird
yet you have declared
you were there first—
is that what I heard?

BARLOW: We were there before the law
of police you must inquire
for the prints in the dust
after we were there prior,

why they say it was hot
when it was a cool place.
and I don't mean the décor
but the air in our face,

and I'll tell you one thing
unlike Brownie and I
the police, and the cops
may have reason to lie,
if they do, I don't know
if they do, ask them why.

KNOWLTON: I am done here, Your Honor,
the re-direct may apply.

JENNINGS: I too have no questions
or any fish left to fry.

JUDGE: Your next witness, Mr. Jennings.

JENNINGS: I call to the stand Mr. Hyman Lubinsky
to continue this vital discussion

let us examine what he has to say
the testimony of this Jewish Russian.

HYMAN LUBINSKY a Russian immigrant, approaches the stand. Dressed smartly, he displays an air of pride and importance, but being an immigrant, with a touch of suspicion.

Direct-examination.

JENNINGS:	Mr. Lubinsky, can you inform the court of the work that you do of the truth you support?
LUBINSKY:	I'm an ice cream peddler of my job that's my scheme with ice flavored milk I sell with my team.
JENNINGS:	By a team do you mean your carriage and horse?
LUBINSKY:	By my team what I mean is a horse, of course.
JENNINGS:	Where do you keep your team can you name the place or stable and of the Borden murder house are you familiar or able?
LUBINSKY:	They are kept at Charlie Gardner's between Morgan and Rodman until the team are needed I work and when I can, and of the Borden house I didn't know at the time it was the murder house of this despicable crime, I wish it were not true that it was not the case but alas here I am where the truth I embrace.
JENNINGS:	On the day of the killings were you selling ice cream

which way did you drive
when you arrived at the scene?

LUBINSKY: I drove towards Second Street
by Andrew Borden's place
I looked over to the yard
where I saw a pretty face,
a lady I noticed walking
with nobility, poise and grace
she walked into the house
where her image was erased.

JENNINGS: When this lady was in the yard
can you tell us what you saw
perhaps what she was wearing
or evidence you may draw?

LUBINSKY: Of her dress and the color
I must say it was very dark
she wore nothing on her head
of that I can remark.

JENNINGS: There are two women in that house
the servant and the Queen
did you ever sell them any
of this fat you call ice cream?

LUBINSKY: Of my wares I have peddled
a new flavor called sardine
though the maid loved vanilla
I could sell it to the Queen,
and of the woman in the yard
that day I had seen
was not the servant or the maid
I can say, cause I'm not green.

JENNINGS: Your witness, Mr. Knowlton,
need to visit the latrine.

JENNINGS walks out of the courtroom, quickly. KNOWLTON approaches the witness.

Cross-examination.

KNOWLTON: Mr. Lubinsky—
you say you sell ice cream

who is your source
and who peddles more product
is it you or your horse?

LUBINSKY: My boss is Mr. Wilkinson
the commander and chief
at 42 North Main Street
where my visits are brief.

KNOWLTON: So—
what is your tale
on that hot street that day
why were you traveling
that route and that way?

LUBINSKY: I did drive up Second Street
with my sweet horse named Mable
where she asks me to be fed
at Charlie Gardner's lovely stable.

KNOWLTON: Hmm! I see—
you went up Second Street
after speaking with your horse
to see one Charlie Gardner
and that hunger was the force,
did you brush down the pony
and his teeth did you floss
tell us where you went soon after
to sell your goods of cream and frost?

LUBINSKY: It was a little after eleven
when I went jingling by
on my trip down Second Street
on my way to Rock and High,
and at the home of Mr. Borden
walking slow a young lady
between the house and the barn
a site that looked warm but shady,
she walked towards the side porch
wearing a dark colored dress
it was not the vanilla servant
of this I can confess.

KNOWLTON: *(Speaking quickly.)*
You went house to house

<table>
<tr><td></td><td>hollering out, "ICE CREAM"
driving down Second Street
when this woman you seen?</td></tr>
<tr><td>LUBINSKY:</td><td>I know not what you say
you ask me much too fast
I am not schooled in English
unless it's for a flavor you ask.</td></tr>
<tr><td>KNOWLTON:</td><td>On the way to the Highlands
once your steed was wined and fed
you looked into the Borden yard
where your intuitions led,
why were you snooping
around for a look
is that your twisted practice
your strategy, your hook?</td></tr>
<tr><td>LUBINSKY:</td><td>I look inside the windows
and when people there are seen
I knock upon the door
and sell them all ice cream,</td></tr>
<tr><td></td><td>whether your desire is vanilla
perhaps chocolate or sorbet
or my favorite, maple walnut
which will surely make your day,</td></tr>
<tr><td></td><td>for it's the best food in the world
it's all me and Mable eat
it makes me feel like a youngster
and refreshes you in the heat,</td></tr>
<tr><td></td><td>so if you are ever on the street
and you see me and my Mable
holler "ice cream, ice cream"
and I'll bring it to your table.</td></tr>
</table>

KNOWLTON walks away from the witness as JENNINGS returns.

<table>
<tr><td>KNOWLTON:</td><td>I am finished, Your Honor
of this witness I have no more
the prosecution rests its case
we surrender the floor.</td></tr>
</table>

JUDGE: Very well then—
Mr. Knowlton, Mr. Jennings.
I need you both to prepare
a clever closing argument
on the floor for us to share.

KNOWLTON: If it pleases the court
I would like to include
a new surprise witness
a pharmaceutical dude,
with some vital affirmation
to which we have reviewed.

JUDGE: Who is your witness
against the accused?

KNOWLTON: It is one Eli Bence
we would like to extrude.

JENNINGS: We object, Your Honor,
the proceedings are over
in addition—
we had previous discussions
of this witness's moreover
and the prosecution agreed
he would not appear or be used
if Your Honor may recall
allegations which were skewed.

JUDGE: Gentlemen, let's discuss this issue
in my chambers right now
and speak of this development
if we are to, or not allow
this witness be brought forward
or any evidence he may vow.

JUDGE and COUNCIL retire to chambers to discuss the appearance of ELI BENCE, an employee at D.R. Smith Pharmacy, who claimed that LIZZIE BORDEN was in his store the day before her parents were killed, and tried to purchase prussic acid, a powerful poison sold by prescription.

The light in the room dims to dark. The focus is now on DARROW and BRYAN at the rear of the room.

DARROW: I call.

DARROW pushes a hand full of matchsticks to the center of the table. BRYAN raises one eyebrow with surprise.

BRYAN: I raise twenty. *(Counts the matches and slides them into the pot.)*

DARROW: *(Looking up at the portrait of Lincoln above BRYAN's head, and smirking.)* I raise you another twenty.

BRYAN: I remind you that we are using matchsticks as money. You realize that if you did not use them to light all those cigarettes or suck on them like candy you would have a lot more to bet with?

DARROW: Never mind that. Just play.

DARROW lights another cigarette. He is bluffing with a losing hand, but has the advantage, since he can see, and is sure of, the cards BRYAN is holding.

BRYAN: So, what is your assessment of Hyman Lubinsky?

DARROW: Detrimental, to say the least.

BRYAN: Bah!

DARROW: Hyman Lubinsky has proven that Liz was at the barn just as she testified at her inquest—to say nothing about how the Russian wrapped Knowlton around his little finger. He also testified that she had on a dark colored dress like the one the prosecution is holding as evidence...the one Liz gave them. And he loves horses. Can't be a bad guy.

BRYAN: How can you infer Lubinsky has them around his finger? The man can just about speak English.

DARROW: Precisely! He's an immigrant. Knowlton pushed him around on the stand. The prosecution came across as being combatant and belligerent. On the other hand Lubinsky appeared quite honest. Knowlton's prejudice of foreigners and Lubinsky's confusion to his ambiguous questioning, unhinged an otherwise well-tempered attorney. Knowlton didn't like the man, and I should add, the testimony given.

BRYAN: We'll see, we'll see. *(Places his bet.)* I raise you another twenty.

DARROW: *(Counting matches carefully.)* And as for Thomas Barlow and Everett Brown, they may have proven the police liars or inept at best. The youth were in that loft. There should have been all sorts of footprints in the floor dust, yet the police refute that fact, stating that no one had been up there in ages.

BRYAN: I don't believe Barlow and Brown. They are just poolroom ruffians.

DARROW: They were perfect young gentlemen. Whether you believe them or not, the ingredient of doubt has been added to the mix, and is simmering in the jurors heads as we speak.

BRYAN: Come on, come on...play.

DARROW: Don't rush me. I'm thinking. Very well, here's your twenty and I raise another thirty.

BYRAN nervously prepares to make a bet, then changes his mind. He studies his competitor who is looking up at the portrait of Lincoln. BYRAN looks back and up over his shoulder then back at DARROW. The cogs in his brain turn ever faster as he is lost in thought.

DARROW: Well...as you put it, play the cards.

BRYAN: *(After a long pause.)* Bah! I fold. *(Slams his cards on the table.)*

DARROW: *(Not showing his cards.)* Aha! Tied! Three games apiece.

BRYAN: Let me see those cards.

DARROW: *(Mixing them back into the deck.)* Sorry old chap...don't need to.

BRYAN: You bluffed that hand, didn't you?

DARROW: That is neither here nor there. What is of importance is that you folded—I won.

BRYAN: Fine, fine. We still have Eli Bence.

DARROW: The earth and sea are full of evils, and once you allow Pandora to wring that lid, the demons released may be more than you can handle.

BRYAN: There you go again, preaching your Greek gibberish. Speak plainly, man.

DARROW: You don't know what skeletons that may be hidden in Eli Bence's closet. They may even still have some flesh on them, for which the defense will carve and feast.

BRYAN: The defense accomplished very little in the way of character abrasion when it came to all the other prosecuting witnesses. I don't see why Bence should be any different. Have you heard something?

DARROW: Only what you and I have read in the newspapers. I don't see how his testimony is pertinent.

BRYAN: Are you serious? She tried purchasing prussic acid, poison, at a druggist.

DARROW: The weapon used to kill those people was a sharp instrument not poison. In any event, she was not sold any and the claim is she walked out without a purchase. His testimony will be expunged as it leaves his lips. He's an unbefitting witness.

BRYAN: If you want to talk about unbefitting witnesses, let's talk about Joseph Lemay. Witness for the defense who claims he saw a man on his property with an axe crying poor, poor, Mrs. Borden.

DARROW: Well, it's true. The man threatened Lemay with an axe. And according to Lemay, the man was covered in blood.

BRYAN: That incident happened twelve days after the crime.

DARROW: And?

BRYAN: And it was four miles away from the Borden house. I don't see what it has to do with anything.

DARROW: Well, if you think Lemay's testimony is inadmissible so is Bence's. Give me Lemay. I know his testimony was omitted. But let him testify and let his declaration stand on it's own merits. I'll give you Bence and you give me Lemay.

BRYAN: Do you really want him to tell his outlandish tale of seeing a blood covered axe–wielding madman almost two weeks after the crime, and half way across town, and in a French accent?

DARROW: No, I suppose not. Well, I don't see how Bence is going to be of any help to you.

BRYAN: Well, here comes the judge and the attorneys. The climax is in the cards. Come, let's play the final hand.

BLACKOUT

ACT III
Scene Two

KNOWLTON and JENNINGS walk back into the courtroom and take their respected places at their desks facing the bench. The JUDGE walks in behind them. The SPECTATORS in the courtroom jump to their feet in applause and with the cheerful roar of jubilation. With a sheepish smile, the JUDGE raises his arms and pats the air around him. They quiet down. He sits. EVERYONE sits back down and the courtroom falls back into tranquility.

BRYAN asks the dealer, DARROW, for two cards. After receiving them, BRYAN smiles and slips them in with the other's in his hand and holds them close to his vest. DARROW tries to spy on BRYAN's hand from the portrait above, but BRYAN holds the cards to close too his body for him to see them.

Direct-examination.

JUDGE: Mr. Knowlton, you may proceed
                      call your next witness
                      as Mr. Jennings agreed.

KNOWLTON: I call on Eli Bence
                      to come forward with speed.

The BAILIFF saunters over, Bible in hand, swears in the witness, ELI BENCE, who is carrying a flute, and promptly prances away.

KNOWLTON: Good afternoon, Sir,
                      tell us your name.

BENCE: Eli Bence last I heard
                      I believe it's still the same.

KNOWLTON: What do you do for a living
                      and where do you work?

BENCE: I'm employed by Mr. Smith
                      as a pharmacist clerk.

KNOWLTON: And where is this place
                      can you please make it plain?

BENCE: It's downtown near Columbia
             at the corner of Main.

KNOWLTON: Now, you know why we're here
             in this courtroom today?

BENCE: You have graciously invited me
             to this legal essay
             that I should become famous
             in this courtroom today
             and I am ready and able
             for your summoned foray
             so on with the hoedown
             get this performance underway.

KNOWLTON: You witnessed Lizzie Borden
             better known as the bad seed
             romp into your store
             for a potion in need.

BENCE: Into my store,
             she did so indeed.

KNOWLTON: Tell us some more,
             please continue,
             proceed.

BENCE: Though they think I have no talent
             that I'm just a little tyke,
             but, I can play a flute soprano
             (pulls out his flute)
             or some piccolo I can strike
             or if it's classical you prefer
             I'll do Mozart if you like.

             I used to do tap dancing
             but I don't do that no more
             the lodger below objected
             to my footwork on the floor
             claimed his ceiling was cracking
             he's still upset and still quite sore
             if you ask me my opinion
             well, he was just a dreary bore.

KNOWLTON: Not now, Mr. Bence,

just tell us about that day
Lizzie Borden came into the store
don't let your tunnel vision stray.

BENCE: It was early one morning
(putting his flute away)
the day before the crime
Miss Borden came a strolling
looking lost, but so divine,

I said—
can I help you there dear lady
she looked suspicious but placid
she replied—
"a dime's worth of a compound
called, Spot-out prussic acid."

You see—
"I have a seal skin cape
with some droppings or some poop
by some birds which flew real low
in a flock or a pooping group.

I'd like to treat the garment
clean off the greasy smear
so I can wear the fur attire
not look dopey and queer."

I said—
we just can't dose out prussic
to any Mary, Joe, or Pete,
a prescription is required
you're not buying bread or wheat,
it's a dangerous medicine
unlike steak beef or pig's feet
you're at a druggist dear madam
not a market in Rome or Crete.

Now if she had asked for laudanum
or some cannabis extract
some codeine or some morphine
for some tooth pain to extract,
we would gladly sell her heroin
for a pain in her neck or back
but not an ounce of prussic acid

it's not like speed or crack,
who did she think she was talking to
the skaters Frick and Frack.

KNOWLTON: Did her temper boil or smolder
did she give you the evil eye
when you gave the cold shoulder
and her request you did deny?

BENCE: She left in a huff and in a puff
and just walked out of the store
and like the wolf and the three pigs
I thought she'd blow down my door.

KNOWLTON: Now—
we know Lizzie killed her mother
that's what we will have proved
that she chopped up her poor daddy
since of him she disapproved,

of the way he spent his money
or the fact he would not budge
to rid them of her stepmother
for which she held a nasty grudge.

JENNINGS: I beg of you Judge—
the witness must not reply
to the affairs at the house
you must exclude and deny,
this sort of interrogation
must not stand on trust, I cry.

JUDGE: Please, Mr. Knowlton,
no rumors or hearsay
stick just to the facts
let your questioning not stray.

KNOWLTON: If it pleases the court
I will reframe, I pray
and ask the question once again
but this time in another way,
is it safe to surmise
and can we all conclude
Lizzie Borden was the woman
you were forced to preclude,

who tried to score some acid
for her parents she subdued?

JENNINGS: Again Your Honor—
this unseemly and leading quiz
questions he tweets and quacks
sounding like a rowdy duck
making a scandal of the facts,
of allegations and assertions
and improper foul attacks.

JUDGE: Play nice, Mr. Knowlton
I will not ask you once more
address the witness another way
and not like you did before.

KNOWLTON: I rest, Your Honor
no more questions
I surrender the floor.

JENNINGS, contemplating, walks slowly toward the witness, rubbing his chin, he begins his reproachable and remonstrative cross-examination.

Cross-examination.

JENNINGS: Now, Mr. Bence—
you are happy to testify
since you think you are a star
to perform for us today
with a flute, now that's bizarre
but however and non-the-less,
by-golly, here you are.

BENCE: Yes, is it not stupendous
that a man such as me
could make all the papers
and I'm sure you'll agree
that this colossal proceeding
this titanic menagerie
will make us all quite famous
like Tweedledum and Tweedledee,
so tell me when you're ready
since I brought my flute with me.

JENNINGS: Mr. Bence, please focus here
there's been a disaster

two people were killed
and sent to their master
with blood spilled all over
on woodwork and plaster.

BENCE: What is the problem, Mr. Lawyer,
do you want me to talk faster?

JENNINGS: Just stick to the details
and what you have seen
like what the woman was wearing
do you know what I mean,
about the color of her dress
was it red, brown, or green?

BENCE: Of the color of her dress
I could not say on that day
but I know it was very dark
but not yellow, red, nor grey.

JENNINGS: Is that dress she has on now
the one she wears today
is that the garment you remember
to the color you portray?

BENCE: No that is not the color
I saw on her that day.

JENNINGS: Do you know Miss Borden
and have you seen her in town?

BENCE: On my way up Main Street
I would see her around.

JENNINGS: Now, did you go to the house
where Lizzie Borden resides
with police as an escort
did you all go inside,
with thirty pieces of silver
with the devil did you confide
to implicate my noble client
is that the fish that you have fried?

BENCE: With officers Doherty and Harrington
I went to the Borden home

they asked Lizzie some questions
I listened for rhythm and tone,
and her voice was quite familiar
with the same tempo and same drone.

JENNINGS: Now think—
was it the same voice
you heard on that day
of the woman who came in
to purchase an acid puree?

BENCE: I stood by the door
as the police talked away
the woman's voice that I heard
was the same from that day,

the one which had inquired
of prussic acid to obtain
for which I did deny her
for which I made it plain
she needed a doctor's prescription
one made out in her full name.

JENNINGS: Mr. Bence, please tell us
are you an expert at speech
of reverberation or pronunciation
of elocution can you teach,

are you a student in lecture
peroration or enunciation
that you say the voices are similar
when you arrive at your accusation?

and that the woman at the drugstore
and Lizzie Borden that you blame
they are both the same creature
and identical as you claim?

BENCE: No, I am not a graduate
in the academy of voice
but I know what I heard
and it leaves me no choice,

I would call her tone tremulous
at the store and at the house

she spoke softly and mutely
like a begging cheesy mouse,

for it was the same woman
at the home where I went
and the pharmacy customer
for which I cannot relent,
or make up a silly story
into a coincidental event.

JENNINGS: I am done, Your Honor
In this case we rest
of Mr. Bence and his flute
and his uncommon request.

JUDGE: Mr. Knowlton, your witness.

KNOWLTON: The State also rests
we stand firm and resolute
to the innocence or guilt
we leave to the jury's pursuit,
all right, Mr. Bence,
go ahead and play your flute.

ELI BENCE quickly pulls out his flute and begins to play "Three Blind Mice,"
while the JUDGE orders him to step down. BENCE walks out of the courtroom
playing the flute as notes fade into silence. The JUDGE shouts out.

JUDGE: That will be all, Mr. Bence,
can you kindly keep it down,
By the way, you're out of key
tune the flute and get out of town.

Gentlemen and counsel—
prepare yourself
for your ultimate speech
closing arguments should be ready
for the jury you must reach,

to prove your case without doubt
the defendant to impeach
or to let her free as a bird
as the jury may well preach,

but if she is found guilty
you may write this down in quote

that a hemp of strong stretch fiber
we will use as a hangman's rope
and snap that golden Borden neck
without expectations, without hope.

At the rear of the room BRYAN takes one last look at his cards and gives DARROW a raised eyebrow. He places his poker hand on the table, face down. Standing, he addresses the court in a loud voice as he quickly walks forward and approaches the bench. DARROW, curious and amused by BRYAN's conduct, leans back in his chair, lights a fresh cigarette, and prepares to appraise his associate's antics.

BRYAN: If it so pleases the court, I William Jennings Bryan, attorney and representative from the great state of Nebraska will give the closing arguments—with your permission, Your Honor.

JUDGE: Do you dispute this intent, Mr. Knowlton?

KNOWLTON: I surrender the floor to my accomplished colleague, Your Honor. A member of the house, a secretary of state, and three-time presidential candidate, surely he has proven his competency.

Closing argument for the prosecution.

BRYAN: May it please the Foreman of the jury, your esteemed Honor, and all acclaimed participants and officials, in conjunction with this most monumental proceeding, that it is not by conquest but by sadness that we determine the guilt of one Lizzie Andrew Borden in the killings of her father and stepmother, and for which I am honored to be allowed to represent the Commonwealth in respectable manner, implementing justice and equity in a fair and speedy means.

On August 4th, 1892, Andrew Jackson Borden and his good wife were butchered in their own home, in the light of day, late morning, while the fair city of Fall River, Massachusetts, went about common everyday responsibilities. No trespasser or perpetrator was witnessed that day by anyone inside or outside that house at 92 Second Street—this while two people were brutally slaughtered, within that modest residence. Most uncommon you may say—most uncommon indeed.

Someone enters a home to commit a heinous crime in a busy neighborhood, does his deed, and exits with clandestine decorum one hour later, even though he is covered in blood and concealing a bloody weapon. Yet no one saw this fiend. How can that be possible, you may ask?

The reason, gentlemen of the jury, is because the killer of those two despairing unfortunates never entered or exited that property, but instead remained there before, during, and after the murders—or more unambiguously, the acrimonious killer lodged there. I assert that person to be one Lizzie Andrew Borden, the daughter of Andrew Borden. As it has been made plain here in this lawful institution, the powerful motive was animosity and greed.

The defendant had a rancor for her stepmother, wanted her gone, and blamed her father for not making such an event occur. She carried inside her heart the vile motive and abominable incentive, dare I add, the induced stimulus to commit such an unthinkable action—along with a burning desire, and a longing determination to feed her depraved and indefensible cravings.

Lizzie Borden yearned for a more preferable life, one in a posh neighborhood on the Hill, and though, through his goodness, and with a loving rectitude, Andrew Borden supplied his daughters with all their essential and supplementary needs, it was not enough for one, Lizzie Borden. Though her father was rumored as having enemies, none have come forward or ever identified.

And if we are to believe that the elderly gentleman did indeed have a dangerous foe, a savage rival, I contended and put before you the resolution that that enemy lived under his very roof. Beelzebub was indeed a woman, Satan, in truth, a daughter—Lizzie Borden.

I have no tenable explanation to why the police may have overlooked certain specifics. After all they are people like you and I. Living their lives and doing their best. But we are dealing here with a well-planned and cunning villain. The evidence of the bloody garment was cleverly hidden by Lizzie Borden somewhere in that house, and the first opportunity she had, she burnt the incriminating evidence, the bloody dress, in the kitchen stove. Even her best friend, the brave and esteemed Alice Russell, believed it to be an infraction and in doing so brought this crucial proof to the proper authorities, witnessed the burning thereof, the bloody dress that was indeed worn by Lizzie Borden when she committed the dastardly deed.

Also, as everyone here has witnessed, the hatchet with the missing handle, which she more than likely broke off and destroyed, was a perfect fit into the gruesome and grotesque wounds in the victims skulls. But let us assume that there could be some possibility that it was not the weapon that felled these two fine people. Then we must assume that she was successful in the disposal of that chilling, egregious instrument.

Let me go as far as to suggest that she strapped the axe to her inner thigh that day, and wore it, until she found an appropriate time, place, or person to dispose of it. Who, here in this courtroom, man or woman, would be prepared to lift and search under a woman's garments? But we know what happened to the bloody dress, and we have in our possession the likely murder weapon, one which she washed of blood and hid away in an old wooden tool box in the basement of that house, hoping it would not be discovered.

I ask you. How can such a crime happen under the nose of two women residing in that house, one washing windows, the other eating pears in the back yard, or looking for sinkers in the barn, ironing handkerchiefs, etc., etc., and not have the least rudimentary view of the killer, who supposedly loitered on the property for the greater part of an hour, killing two people in the interim?

That, my friends, is because Lizzie Borden is a killer and a liar. She lied about her stepmother receiving a note, and she lied about going to the barn to look for sinkers. Instead, she had committed the heinous act of murder upon her own stepmother, and with forethought and prudent anticipation, waited over an hour, and then perpetrated the same upon her loving father. This after an attempt to poison them failed. What poison had she tried, you may ask. It was not one which exposed itself in the predominant autopsies of the deceased, for none was found.

And true, tests did not show the use of prussic acid. But you all heard the undisputed testimony of Eli Bence. The fact that Lizzie Borden attempted the purchase of such a deadly compound the day before the gruesome deaths of her parents, though circumstantial, stands with indisputable plausibility and fused suspicion.

This she tried explaining away as a remedy needed to clean a seal skin cape. A seal skin cape indeed. She is a calculative assassin. This she exposes with her cold, austere and unsympathetic temperament, one that only a callous and unemotional killer could display. Indirect proof you may indicate— Conjectural and inconclusive? Perhaps! But these comprehensive and explicit actions are the calculative measures of a culpable and skilled killer.

The math does not dissimulate the evidence at hand.

> Lizzie Borden took an axe
> and gave her mother nineteen whacks
> and when she discovered what she had done
> she gave her father ten plus one.

This is the only conclusion left to you. Lizzie Borden must atone for her actions, and I ask that you find her guilty of the murders of Abby and Andrew Borden. Thank you.

EVERYONE in the courtroom stands in what is now very familiar applause and ovation. There are a few "bravos" and "well saids," with one or a handful of hecklers. The JUDGE bangs his gavel. EVERYONE sits back down and comes to order. The only sound left is that of DARROW, who stands at the rear of the courtroom, clapping his hands. The JUDGE calls for the defense to mount its rebuttal and closing argument. As BRYAN returns to the card table, DARROW starts for the bench at the head of the room before JENNINGS could take the floor.

DARROW: Your Honor, with permission from the defense I would like to effectuate the closing argument, if I may be so permitted?
JUDGE: I have no objections—you Mr. Jennings?
JENNINGS: I have no protest, Your Honor. Besides, I need to use the...

Looking somewhat desperate, ANDREW JENNING leaves the room in haste to satisfy a visit to the restroom.

JUDGE: That is settled then. Proceed, Mr. ah?
DARROW: To those who do not know me, my name is Clarence Seward Darrow. I am a member in good standing with the American Civil Liberties Union, which I am certain no one has heard of. But believe me, it is an ethical and upstanding organization, if not a futuristic one. As a defense lawyer and honored civil libertarian, I will stand in for Mr. Jennings, while he tends to much more urgent duties.

EVERYONE in the courtroom begins to laugh, including the JUDGE, who bangs his gavel.

DARROW: And in doing so I will prove to you without skepticism, without mistrust, or apprehension, and above all, without doubt, the innocence of Miss Liz.

Now, you have heard quite a bit during this trial about blood evidence, about the murder weapon, and women's fashion, particularly color, which to a man has little noteworthiness, unless it is the color of his ale.

There are a few chuckles.

Whether the dress the prosecution has in its possession today was worn on the day of the crime or not, we can be certain of one thing. It is free of blood, and that the police found no garment in that entire house with blood on it. Some have speculated that the murders were committed by my genial client while she was—excuse the expression—naked, and thus the blood was easily washed away. That my friends is the fabric of fiction, or of a man who does not recognize the color of a good stout ale, or perhaps has had one too many ales.

The COURTROOM breaks into laughter. The JUDGE bangs his gavel and restores order.

JUDGE: Omit the humorous analogies and metaphors, Mr. Darrow.
DARROW: Sorry, Your Honor.
JUDGE: Proceed.
DARROW: Now there was no blood found on my client. Not a dot, a speckle... or even a pinprick, from any of the victims. As you have discovered, listening to vigorous and exceptional testimony, from one witness after another, from both the prosecution and the defense, that there is no possibility that the offender could have escaped the drenching that the lacerating instrument rained down on him.

Then there is the story about the infamous sick note. That Liz lied about the note, which was delivered to her stepmother, has no merit. One cannot demonstrate that it did or did not exist, was or was not delivered, or that Abby Borden did not destroy it after she received it. It does not prove falsehood, show deception, or has it any relevance to the existing crime. The actuality that the prosecution may evaluate the defendant's integrity by an enigmatic piece of parchment is preposterous.

Let us talk about Liz and the accusations that she had lied about going to the barn. When in fact, her walk to the barn was corroborated by Mr. Hyman Lubinsky to be an actuality. Allegations that she did not go to the barn to look for sinkers or some iron and, while there, had not eaten pears, has been proven erroneous. As a matter of fact it was fallacious, when it is proven by a third party, one who has no valid profit or gain in testifying to a falsehood, that Liz was indeed seen in the yard, or coming from the barn, as she testified to at the inquest, when her father was being killed. What more endorsement is needed?

Now, our protectors the police, testified that no one was up in the barn, because they could discover no footprints on what they described as a dusty floor—or that the heat in the barn was too oppressive for anyone to spend any significant time there. Yet Thomas Barlow and Everett Brown testified that it was in fact a cool place, and that they had dallied in the loft and in the hay, on the dust, in the dust, with the dust. A cool place.

Why did police not see the footprints left by Barlow and Brown who were there previous? What could be the reason for Brown and Barlow's audacious deception? What do these two young men gain by giving fallacious testimony? Members of the jury, make no mistake. Someone is perpetrating a falsehood here. Or, let us call it what it is. A lie!

Could it be the authorities, who through sequestered shame for their precipitous ineptitude, or by an inability to steer this investigation in the right direction, thus bungling this case, the people we must question? Give this further thought. Are police not akin to standing dominoes? If one gets it wrong and is pushed over, will not the rest of them follow— tuck themselves closely behind their comrades, each one repeating the same inaccuracy, unwilling to defy the group? I suppose I am speaking about deep-seated principles here, fundamental to the uniform and how it is perceived by a law abiding public.

But we can see behind the glass, and just because it is frosted does not mean we are totally blind. Errors were made here, perhaps errors in good faith. Don't forget the old fable about where roads paved in good faith and intentions lead.

If the law says the sky is green, should we believe it? Are all public servants official and honest? Does the badge they wear pierce their hearts to the wall of high-mindedness and fair play? I'm afraid only you can answer that. But this much is true. You must ask yourself these questions. Consider what may be obvious.

As for the hatchet. It was substantiated and corroborated by the prosecution's own witness, the doctor for the State, that it was impossible to completely wash blood from the broken wood handle which protruded from the handless axe, for which my esteemed colleague, Mr. Knowlton, submitted as an exhibit, as if to imply that it was the murder weapon, since they had none. Not only was it not the murder weapon, but a very common instrument, one used in every household, for cutting kindling and other minor tasks. A tool. Not a weapon after all. Should we be surprised by its existence? No.

Now if I may be so blunt as to remind the court that Andrew and Abby Borden were killed with a razor sharp instrument, not prussic acid. Can the prosecution produce a seal skin cape which it contends Liz was going to clean with prussic acid? Was a seal skin cape ever discovered and confiscated? Has it been proven one way or another that she ever owned a seal skin cape? Is there anyone else who can collaborate what Eli Bence has accused my client of? Members of the jury, does prussic acid really have any credence in these murders?

You must ask yourself one and all these questions. And you will arrive at only one conclusion. No! It does not.

Though Bridget Sullivan testified that everyone in the house was ill at the time of the crime, was any poison discovered in the stomachs of Abby and Andrew Borden? No! It was not. I concur, according to the State Examiners, no toxins or contaminates were found in the organs of the dearly departed. Let us not forget or get distracted by the prussic acid issue. That is not how the victims were killed. Mr. Bence's testimony is inconsequential. It must be thrown out.

Now we don't need to be special investigators or crime detectives to sort out the facts here. It is elementary. This case can be easily measured by the simple passage of time. Let us look at Andrew Borden, just before the time he had his life snuffed out. A study of the clock alone will prove that it was impossible for Liz...

DARROW looks at BRYAN at the rear of the courtroom who is smiling and looking confident and smug. DARROW's argument becomes more heated. He begins to address LIZZIE BORDEN by her proper name.

DARROW: No, allow me to rephrase—impossible for Lizzie Andrew Borden to commit this abominable outrage—the murder of a loving father and a mother who had taken care of her since she was a child.

Andrew Borden was last seen alive by Bridget Sullivan, a couple of minutes before 11:00 a.m., as she completes the washing of the dining room windows. After Bridget was done with her chores she washed out her bucket and rags and decided to go up to her room to take a short nap. Again, it is known that this occurred sometime before eleven in the morning, perhaps five minutes or so before. Bridget Sullivan maintained that she was not in her room that long, and had just laid her head down when she heard the city hall clock sound, just down the street. Furthermore, she looked up at her own clock and noticed that it was 11:00 a.m. Bridget maintains that the total time she spent in her room was ten, or perhaps, fifteen minutes at most, before Lizzie called her back downstairs, stating, and I quote, "Come down quick, father's dead, somebody came in and killed him." Let me say that again. "Somebody came in and killed him."

Measuring by father-time, we learn that from the moment Bridget Sullivan had seen Andrew Borden alive, to the minute Lizzie Borden summoned her, very little time had passed. If in fact it was true, Lizzie Borden had ten to fifteen minutes to kill her father, wash herself off, and rid herself of the blood soaked clothing, and cause the hatchet to vanish—if we are to believe she is to be accused of this crime.

Doubtful! Implausible! And dare I utter, nearly impossible! Even if she had the time to bathe all the blood away, groom her bloody hair, and place on clean clothing... what happened to the axe, the cleaver, the hatchet? Where did it go? Did she carve one from a block of ice and let it just melt away? After all we know it was a hot day. Did she drop it down into the commode—serve it with mutton stew? Don't be preposterous, you say. I agree. Let's not. To accuse my client of this crime is just that.

An army of police searched the property at 92 Second Street and never found the murder weapon. Let me repeat—never found the murder weapon. Why? Because the real killer took it away when he left the property.

Now, ask yourself, why did Bridget not report that the clothing Lizzie had on before the murder was not the same clothing fifteen minutes later? Because it was. There was no blood on her dress because she did not kill anyone.

I will not insult you by entertaining the possibility that the hatchet, which sits here in this courtroom today, the one with the broken handle, is the murder weapon. I know it is not. You know it is not. The doctor knows it is not. Alas, the State knows it is not. So why is it here—what are we left with... doubt, undisputed uncertainty, skepticism, and the inadequate attempt at circumstantial validation?

DARROW walks up to the JUROR and looks him in the eye, while pointing at LIZZIE BORDEN.

DARROW: Are you prepared to hang that woman on such insubstantial and chintzy evidence? Who is prepared to slip the noose over her guiltless locks, unfasten the button of her blouse, and constrict the loop of death tightly around the fair skin of that virtuous neck?

DARROW walks along the front of the courtroom pointing at REPORTERS, COURT OFFICIALS, and SPECTATORS. Shouting.

DARROW: You? You? How about you?
JUDGE: *(Banging his gavel.)* Mr. Darrow, address the bench and the jury. The press and onlookers are of no concern or part of these proceedings.
DARROW: Just trying to make a point, Your Honor. One of civil liberty and the right thereof. Allow me to continue and ask... are we all barbarians? Must we descend to the contemptible level of the assassin to obtain

justice and righteousness? And if so, think of the savagery and the philistinism in the unjust punishment we may inflict on an innocent defendant, if we are in error. *(Looking up at BRYAN.)* May your God forgive us.

Remember that in the English language the term defendant, or the phrase accused, are not euphemisms for criminal or offender. *(Pondering.)*

But just a moment. I lecture on the possibility of guilt where no guilt exists... for the sake of argument, you understand. I am confident that as I speak... this very moment... the constitution and integrity of one Lizzie Andrew Borden is being restored in the minds of every good citizen in this room... in this county—hell, in this vast, wonderful country of ours.

Allow me to be outspoken and boldly declare that the State has nothing. If allegations were a stitch in time the babe would be stillborn. If the prosecution's evidence were a gale, in all jurisprudence, it would not blow hard enough to tumble a dry withered leaf along the ground of justice, let alone bend the branch on the tree of impartiality. The faulty evidence submitted to this court does not even reach the fundamental level of doubt, that is to imply, that no doubt is required in a case where innocence and irreproachability reign supreme.

From the start of their investigation the police chased the wrong ferret, climbed down the wrong hole, kicked in the wrong door, and when they discovered that they wasted precious time, the first forty-eight hours, and could still not produce a villain, that they had no suspect, no case, they assembled and fabricated one, trying to make a monster out of my client, one which even Mary Shelley herself could not fashion if she were given all the parchment and ink in the world. And because they have little understanding of my gentle client's character, whether it is her eccentricity, her management of grief, her foible approach to authority, they single her out as the best possible choice for someone to convict in a botched and mishandled investigation.

And as for my distinguished counsel, Mr. William Jennings Bryan, who appears to have taken to the poetry of doggerel, let me recite it as I see it.

> Massachusetts took the law,
> with deception they did draw,
> with subversion they had built,
> a veil of fraud of mire and guilt.

I respectfully implore this court to end this travesty, this clutch on justice. Let us advocate on the side of contrition and return this fine woman her just due dignity, restore her respect, and peacefully send her home... innocent of all charges. Innocent, innocent, innocent. This you must do. I yield.

DARROW starts his long walk back to the card table at the rear or the room. As he does, it is as if he did not speak at all. Strangely and eerily all is silent. But that silence is soon broken by the gavel in the JUDGE's hand.

JUDGE: The court address the juror
                    clerk, Bailiff, make yourself ready
                    look upon the accused
                    less she needs to be held steady.

DARROW sits down and picks up his cards. JENNINGS waits, looking complacent. His cards are held close to his vest. He smiles and pushes all his matchsticks into the pot. DARROW realizes he does not have enough to call. He looks down at his hand. He holds a straight flush. A sure winning hand in almost any game. But this is not just any game. DARROW begins to panic.

BRYAN: Should not have smoked all those cigarettes, Clarence. You must call, raise, or fold, and I can see only one option.

DARROW: Wait, wait, I....

BRYAN: Game is over, Clarence. All your matchsticks are in the pot and you still fall short.

DARROW: No, no, you can't.... wait. My watch. My Grandfather's gold pocket watch. You always admired it. Here, here. It must be worth at least a hundred thousand matchsticks. It must not end this way. *(Drops it onto the mound of matchsticks.)*

BRYAN: We had set rules, Darrow. *(Holds and admires the watch.)* Matchsticks for money. Nothing was said about the use of supplementary funds, let alone jewelry.

DARROW: That's not jewelry. It's a watch. Time. The most valuable commodity held by mankind. *(Pause.)* Afraid, are we, Bryan?

BRYAN: Me... afraid of what, my good man? *(Drops the watch back down on the table.)*

DARROW: That if we play the cards to fruition that my hand will trump yours, and Lizzie Borden will walk free.

BRYAN: Oh, I am very satisfied with the cards I hold, Clarence. I'll tell you what— I'm so confident that I will allow your pocket watch into the pot. It will only make winning that much sweeter.

DARROW looks up at the portrait of Abraham Lincoln which hangs above

BRYAN's head and squints. A symbolic shadow of a hangman's noose now reflects on the wall beside it. DARROW studies his cards and looks over at BRYAN's hands.

BRYAN: Not this time, Clarence.
DARROW: I never considered you as a man to bluff, Bryan.
BRYAN: I suppose there is always a first time for everyone.

In the background, the proceedings approach a climax.

BAILIFF: *(Looking bleak and saddened.)* Lizzie Andrew Borden, stand up.
JUDGE: Jurors, have you reached a verdict?
BRYAN: Bluffing at cards, Clarence, and bluffing at life requires equal fortitude. It's not how you win, but how well you lose that reveals the integrity in us all. Both you and I think we hold the model of victory in our hands. One of us is wrong, and to the victor goes the fate of one Lizzie Borden.
DARROW: But of course.

DARROW spreads his cards on the table and displays a grin. A six, seven, eight, nine, and a ten. A straight flush, all in hearts. At the head of the courtroom the JUROR replies to the JUDGE in a loud, dissenting tone.

JUROR: We have, Your Honor.
BAILIFF: *(Quietly sniveling and sobbing.)* Lizzie Andrew Borden, hold up your right hand and please remain where you stand. Mr. Foreman, look upon the prisoner, prisoner look upon the foreman. What say you, Mr. Foreman?

BRYAN slowly spreads his cards on the table, as he shakes his head with unpleasurable satisfaction. An ace, king, queen, jack, and a ten all in spades. A royal flush. The ultimate winning hand. At the head of the courtroom the JUROR shouts out.

JUROR: We find the defendant GUILTY!

There is a gasp from EVERYONE in the room, voices hum, and murmurs get louder by the second. DARROW jumps out of his chair and begins to shout.

DARROW: No, no... this can't be! It is not the way it is supposed to end. You can't just change history.
BRYAN: Was this not what I set out to do, Clarence?

BRYAN puts on his coat, looks up at the portrait of Abraham Lincoln, then down at DARROW, with displeasure. He shakes his head and walks out of the courtroom, making certain to take DARROW's gold watch with him. LIZZIE BORDEN looks as defiant as ever. DARROW runs up to the bench. EVERYONE ignores him.

DARROW: *(Addressing the court.)* Stop! Now! This verdict must be reversed.

The BAILIFF takes hold of LIZZIE BORDEN's arm and walks her by DARROW on her way out to prison. The room is silent. LIZZIE stops and looks over at DARROW.

DARROW, looking dejected, lowers his head. The light in the room darkens. The only light in display is on LIZZIE BORDEN.

LIZZIE: After all this
        I am left to weep
        on an August black day
        upon a pond of blood
        in the mid-summer hotness
        my thoughts rage and swirl,
        thoughts I dare not speak
        leaving me lost
        lost in a lost world.

LIZZIE looks at a light which brightens across the room. It shines down on the image of ANDREW JACKSON BORDEN, just standing there looking back at her. She sees him, is shocked, and turns away, not quite sure what to do. She recites.

LIZZIE: How could you not see
        the embers of discontent
        which we all flamed
        the stench of fidelity, discarded
        left burning at your feet.

        How you could have been so blind
        why you could have not seen
        when times were good
        and benevolence lean.

        Father, why is it
        you could not foretell
        the fleeting love
        that all was not well,
        of crashing waves
        the bursting, the swells

of longing and need
and vile desperate yells
which you would not feed
which we could not sell
which you would not heed
the damnation of hell.

Now all this love
I'm left to weep
late in life
I'm made to sweep
from room to room
from heart to head
distrust to gloom
of confirmation unsaid
I should have asked of you
but which was best unsaid.

And forever and a day
this infliction will stay
never to be swept
completely away
the question, the answer
I dare not ask.

And I sat forced to choose
between you and her
trying not to lose
what I never did have
the ring which I gave
to you and not me
a daughter's confession
will not come from the grave
leaves me to wonder
be still and behave.

And I'm left with thoughts
that rage and swirl
Father's devotion
he did not choose to unfurl
leaves me lost
lost in a lost world.

LIZZIE looks back at the image of her FATHER who was standing across the room, but it is gone. She looks back at EMMA. A solitary light illuminates EMMA's saddened face, then fades to darkness. LIZZIE reflects on EMMA's long life, one spent caring for her as if she were her mother and begins to sing, "Sweet Emma," a song she sung when she was a little girl.

LIZZIE: Sweet Emma, sweet Emma,
               your graces are but a hidden mist
               a vapor in the morning glow
               fading in damp August heat
               as tears begin to gently flow—for
               no one sees you
               no one needs you
               but me, Lizzie.

               Beat Emma, beat Emma,
               your chest in kiss'n betrayal
               in parched slumber weeping
               a stiff wounded cry
               of stale fading years
               forever asking why—why
               no one sees you
               no one needs you
               but me, Lizzie.

               Sleep, Emma, sleep, Emma,
               dream of days in the Eden sun
               hope for a better life
               the only offering you can
               within a soul in disarray
               with only paradise at hand—where
               no one sees you
               no one needs you
               but me, Lizzie.

               Oh, sweet Emma, sweet Emma,
               ease your mind, anneal your heart
               knead your dreams one upon another
               and forge your parental yearnings
               and chart a soft migration
               before too late the burnings—and
               no one sees me
               no one needs me
               not even, Emma.

DARROW: Have faith, Lizzie Borden. We will appeal this verdict. We will assemble the best legal minds and fight this conviction. If we need search the entire country.

LIZZIE looks at DARROW with suspicion and hope—then down and away.

LIZZIE: Yes, the country. How I love the country.
                  (She pauses.)
                  I yearn for father's farm in Swansea
                  where the maples grow old
                  down Gardners Neck by the sea
                  by the tepid river Cole
                  which flows deep into my veins
                  to the blisters on my soul
                  the reins to my destiny
                  to the woods brave and bold.

                  That small white Cape
                  its bleached shutters bake
                  fanning the summer sun
                  where I was free to dance, to run
                  this farm and these fields
                  my escape it should become
                  away from a cobblestone crowd
                  and locked dwelling doors
                  where the black fallen rain
                  was a soot of discontent
                  from a gray darkened heart
                  where I hide, where I vent
                  my worry and my woe.

                  To Ocean Grove I did resign
                  with bamboo, hook and iron
                  found in a Second Street barn
                  I cast out this weight, this twine
                  which strangles me
                  and into a salty bay
                  I would count the years and weigh
                  the measures I must take
                  to cast my fears away
                  to fish under the Swansea sun.
                  In a fine and jubilant place
                  my inhibitions I always chase
                  down hushed country lanes
                  where I can drown my despair

and spurn all this dread
let the wind unfurl my hair
on that Ocean Grove cove
down the Gardner's Neck Road
at my dear Swansea lair.

DARROW: Yes, Lizzie. That is what you must do. Be strong. Think good thoughts, comforting thoughts. You will see Swansea again. You will see many Swanseas. You will have that big house you always yearned for.

DARROW rests his hand under LIZZIE's elbow and gives her arm a squeeze.

DARROW: You will have your Maplecroft in the sun, Lizzie, you will. I have seen it.

LIZZIE looks down at DARROW's hand, then up to his face, pulling her arm away. She gives him a strange and starry stare. Her mind wanders. A slight smile washes across her lips.

LIZZIE: Maplecroft... yes, yes,
            my Maplecroft in the sun
            where I will no longer need pretend
            or accept it all in trade
            for father and his grave.

            Some blood that day did spill
            when outrage persuaded will
            when honor replaced disgrace
            and scorn I did embrace.

            To procure for me what's mine
            by committing such a crime
            from all those convinced I lied
            to Maplecroft is where I'll hide
            and in Eden make her my bride.

            And the bars that circle this temple
            from a past life will never resemble
            this prison I'm bound to conceal
            the sadness, the cold I feel
            where my heart is prepared to heal.

            In Jerusalem is as it should be
            from a Second Street desert I'll free
            from a Borden lackluster and love
            to my Canaan my Highland above

my desires and dreams I fulfill
to live in a meadow high and still
to sleep like a babe upon a green lawn
and discard the old life, again to be born
to live all my days alone is my will
in a Maplecroft garden high on the hill.

LIZZIE pauses and thinks. She continues her dream of the future.

LIZZIE: I will rest above my garden
on that sterile brash hill
while the western horizon
burns with desire.

I will peer out the window
past the glass and the sill
on damping silk sheets
a crypt craving fire.

But,
how long must I linger
how long must I spend
on French's hill
waiting for love,
to yearn, to hope
a lover to mend
to touch and caress
below and above.

A prince, a knight
inamorata to pursue
hard pressed breasts
to cradle my head
fecundate my seed
a womb sharing two
entwine as one
and grace my bed.

In that kingdom I'll build
by the shade of the day
I'll bloom as a flower
forlorn, I will grow
by the evening dim light
naked I'll lay
still I require

sweet kisses to flow
to set this platter ablaze
kindle this my needs
that hunger to burn
thus, ambers of iron
for a heart made wrought
will rust when it bleeds
cumber of my choosing
on that Maplecroft Zion.

The BAILIFF takes LIZZIE BORDEN by the arm and leads her away. DARROW shouts out to her.

DARROW: Lizzie, keep warm your desires, your aspirations, ambitions, your dreams. I will not forget you. You will be free. We will fight this together.

LIZZIE turns and addresses DARROW.

LIZZIE: Together, Mr. Darrow?
Together?
I think not—
and I'll tell you why...
you are a lawyer.
you have lost this case, Sir
and I... I am on my way to hell.

Like a wandering moon
in pursuit of a retreating sun
you and I will never
rise together.

In the dark side of your world
on the burning surface of my passion
we can only eclipse one another
for the light you shed
is not yours to give
and the warmth reflected
only to the laughing stars
in twinkling chuckles
lost in space and time.

I can only leave you singed,
and with your altering faces
wandering the heavens

it will only leave me with
pucks and craters—
barren and cold—
clinging to the dark side
of your mind and heart,
the undiscovered country
where even you have not gone
where I can never go
or wish to be.

Together?
You see, Mr. Darrow,
do you understand now,
as my counsel you were in alliance
with my essence, in coalition with my desires,
and like father, we were never fiery lovers
your heart never a trinket or latch for my needs
and though you think you have done your best
your edict was never indispensable,
your venture barren and infertile
and in the end, expendable
for you see,
you have lost this case, Mr. Darrow,
and I... well,
I am on the way to hell.

The BAILIFF takes LIZZIE BORDEN out of the darkened room. LIZZIE is gone. The only light shines down on DARROW, who ponders all the words she had spoken.

DARROW: Ungrateful bitch! *(He whispers to himself, lighting a cigarette.)* Patrick Eugene Prendergast was a picnic to defend in place of this woman. She reminds me of my first wife. *(Scratches and shakes his head, placing on his straw hat.)* I suppose I had it coming. I should have never lost this case. I was certain my closing argument was brilliant. Oh well, I suppose it's the bitch inside her which gives her strength. Shouldn't knock what I don't understand, otherwise I would be knocking every woman that ever lived. What in hell went wrong? Still can't determine how Bryan manifested such a winning hand.

BLACKOUT

ACT III
Scene Three

*CLARENCE DARROW walks out of the courtroom where he
finds BRYAN on the courthouse steps watching the CROWD
as they celebrate. EURIPIDES stands by talking with him.
His tone is heated, as he admonishes WILLIAM JENNINGS
BRYAN for changing history. BRYAN tries his best to ignore
EURIPIDES.*

EURIPIDES: Well done, son of Nevada,
               you've changed the hand of time
               it's now the moment to rejoice
               upon spoils of war you'll dine.

               But be not so complacent
               by the card in which you held
               or rejoice in gotten fortunes
               for the tree in which you felled
               for if your God was watching
               your reward may be withheld.

*DARROW walks over. BRYAN turns his back to EURIPIDES, harboring guilt or
shame. EURIPIDES turns and addresses the CROWD in the courtyard.*

EURIPIDES: By the jarring hand
               of inclusive innocence
               she struggles at the helm
               colliding with retribution
               in a storm of putrid justice
               along a cankered realm,

               and with the cinder of rectitude
               where vacuous love simmers
               impregnable with encrusting salt
               still a heart sails moist and glimmers,

               and with a tarnished rusted soul
               tempered by social jaundice
               within an enigmatic world
               left vacant by splintered calmness,
               where unlike the goddess Hera
               she will never grace a bed

---

a destiny lacking warriors
is an infertile lover's thread,

with sacrifices swept away
unlike Alcestis, in a barren cradle
was once a place where gold and wealth
poured free from a silver ladle
this she will have no sight again
or stroll upon a flaxen shore
beyond the marbled levee
where she has a life no more,

and like the wounds of Telephus
her spirit may never heal
to seek and beg redemption
a restitution she can not steal,
to extinguish the bloody flames
and temper her resolve
she must never try to unravel
that... which can't be solved,
as she descends the sanguine Styx
for the sins she can't absolve.

DARROW walks up to EURIPIDES, lowers and shakes his head in remorse for losing the case. Though not angered, EURIPIDES is saddened by the verdict. Feeling a little sorrow for DARROW it is mingled with some displeasure.

EURIPIDES: A tranquil sun sets orange
where it will rage and ignite
by a ruling without equal
in this courtroom tonight.

Where is your breath, young Darrow,
did you leave it by the sand
let it blow out to sea
from your heart, through your hand.

Though you have done your finest
of a good man I cannot ask
to witness Troy blazing
sit by its heat and bask.

When this glory that is justice
though the verdict wears a mask

of a gale that puffs fury
where retribution we cast.

Stretching out arms, EURIPIDES addresses the CROWD in the courtyard once again.

EURIPIDES: So rejoice, all you good people,
in your minds the worm has shaped
like my Cassandra's belated crown
which the law has abused and raped.

And to the rules of this great land
justice always wins in the end
a sack of mire we've been sold
when our virtues they amend.

For the proof is in the pudding
for a blind man's lost his taste
and believes he is unworthy
a law of wrath and haste.

This damsel they have punctured
with their scepter honed but soiled
lancing hearts of all good matrons
when Lizzie's name was spoiled.

EURIPIDES addresses CLARENCE DARROW directly, begging him not to give up on the cause of womanhood, and in doing so, save LIZZIE BORDEN.

EURIPIDES: I beg of you, good servant,
let not prophecy be key
or Apollo spit into her mouth
make pregnant the law's decree.

We must darn this guilt she bears
and muster all the strength that yields
and let all beguiling women sleep
by the rivers of Elysian Fields.

As for Lizzie Andrew Borden
and Deianira's name she claims
with the strength of God and Hercules
you must break these destructive chains.
For it was not fair to meddle
with history's written prayer

if so we must kill all lawyers
for Hades they bring down to bear.

EURIPIDES walks away leaving DARROW to consider the words he'd spoken.

DARROW: You know, Bryan... I'm not much on poetry, but I believe he just insulted us.
BRYAN: It's a reflection, Clarence. We insult ourselves.
DARROW: What do you mean?

There's a long pause. BRYAN takes the cigarette from DARROW's hand and takes a puff.

BRYAN: You cheated.
DARROW: I what?
BRYAN: You heard me, you cheated. You had full view of my cards in the glass, the reflection in the portrait of Lincoln above my head.
DARROW: When did you know?
BRYAN: Oh, it took me a while.
DARROW: All the more reason why we need to do it again, Bryan.
BRYAN: Do what again?
DARROW: An appeal, my good colleague, an appeal. We must play another hand.
BYRON: Oh, no, not me.
DARROW: Don't you see, Bryan. This is wrong. What I did was wrong.
BYRON: It was your idea in the first place.
DARROW: Yes, but think. You are a man of principle. I know you. Fairness and impartiality are not just concepts to be discussed, doctrines to be studied, they are part of your religion.
BYRAN: There you go again, bringing up religion.
DARROW: All right! But think on this. If Lizzie Borden hangs, will you be able to live with yourself?
BRYAN: *(Long pause.)* I don't know... I suppose not. Damn Greek.
DARROW: So?
BRYAN: Just one hand—no more. *(Flings cigarette away.)*
DARROW: If you say so—just one hand. Oh, but what a glorious hand it will be!

DARROW and BRYAN walk along the courthouse stoop stopping just short of the front door. DARROW stops to address BRYAN on a slippery matter.

DARROW: Listen, Bryan, tell me something.
BRYAN: What's that?
DARROW: How the hell did you pull out a royal flush—the odds against

that are tremendously unlikely, especially at that moment of time, and under those circumstances, life and death. It was brilliant.

BRYAN reveals a pack of cards from his pocket.

DARROW: What are those?

BRYAN: It's a spare pack of cards. I had them all along. When I realized that you had been cheating I did a little cheating of my own. While you were giving your closing arguments, the royal flush was ready made.

DARROW: You... cheated?

BRYAN: Yes. And that is the only reason I am giving you a second chance. That and the words of that damn Greek.

DARROW: *(Smiling.)* Why you swindling little bastard!

BRYAN: You may be right there. After all, we are attorneys.

DARROW and BRYAN laugh and start for the courtroom door.

BRYAN: This time you sit under the portrait of Lincoln.

DARROW: Agreed. *(Placing his arm around BYRAN.)* Hey, listen. Do you think I can have my watch back?

BYRAN: Only time will tell, Clarence, time will tell.

CLARENCE DARROW opens the courtroom door and gracefully ushers BRYAN in. The door slams behind them. As the scene ends, suddenly the roar of applause, cheers, and whistling of the SPECTATORS can be heard inside as it starts all over again.

CURTAIN

10595710R00091

Printed in Great Britain
by Amazon